Empire of Ancient Greece

JEAN KINNEY WILLIAMS

☑®

Facts On File, Inc.

Great Empires of the Past: EMPIRE OF ANCIENT GREECE

History Consultant: John W.I. Lee, assistant professor, Department of History, University of California, Santa Barbara

Special thanks to Michael Burgan for his assistance.

Facts On File, Inc.
132 West 31st Street
New York NY 10001

Library of Congress Cataloging-in-Publication Data:
Williams, Jean Kinney.
Empire of ancient Greece / Jean Kinney Williams.
p. cm. – (Great empires of the past)
Includes bibliographical references and index.
ISBN 0-8160-5561-0 (hardcover)
1. Greece–History–To 146 B.C.–Juvenile literature. 2.
Greece–Civilization–To 146 B.C.–Juvenile literature. I. Title. II. Series.
DF215.W58 2005
938–dc22   2004024952

Produced by the Shoreline Publishing Group LLC
Editorial Director: James Buckley Jr.
Series Editor: Beth Adelman
Designed by Thomas Carling, Carling Design, Inc.
Photo research by Dawn Friedman, Bookmark Publishing
Index by Nanette Cardon, IRIS

Wolfgang Kaehler 2004, www.wkaehlerphoto.com: 4, 21, 35; Bridgeman Art Library: 6; Koji Sasahara/AP/Wide World Photos: 10; Carol Phelps/AP/Wide World Photos: 2; Bildarchiv Preussischer Kulturbesitz/Art Resource, NY: 14; The Art Archive/National Archaeological Museum Athens/Dagli Orti: 16; Warner Bros./The Kobal Collection/Bailey, Alex: 19; Thanassis Stavrakis/AP/Wide World Photos: 25; With permission of the Royal Ontario Museum, © ROM: 28; Scala/Art Resource, NY: 33, 68, 87, 116; The Granger Collection, New York: 40, 52, 58; Alinari/Art Resource, NY: 43; The Art Archive/Dagli Orti (A): 46; Archive Photos/Hulton Archive/Getty Images: 57; Bibliotheque Nationale, Paris, France, Archives Charmet/Bridgeman Art Library: 63; Erich Lessing/Art Resource, NY: 64, 81, 83, 105; HIP/Scala/Art Resource, NY: 72; Réunion des Musées Nationaux/Art Resource, NY: 76; The Art Archive/Harper Collins Publishers: 90; Robbie Jack/Corbis: 94; Nimatallah/Art Resource, NY: 99; North Wind Picture Archives: 100; Joel Saget/AFP/Getty Images: 110; Graham Barclay, BWP Media/Getty Images: 119

CONTENTS

Introduction

THE TERM "ANCIENT GREEKS" CAN REFER TO MANY CULTURES and times in world history. The ancient Greeks include the warriors who fought in the Trojan War in the 1200s B.C.E. and whose mythical stories, retold by Homer, are considered the foundation of Western literature. They also are the sophisticated (from the Greek word *sophos*, which means "wisdom") Athenians of what is known as Classical Greece, who gave us democracy in the 400s B.C.E. and whose architecture and literature remain an important part of our culture. And they are the Mediterranean peoples who, in the two centuries before Rome began its rule of the Western and near Eastern world in the 140s B.C.E., made ground-breaking contributions to science and mathematics.

The history of the ancient Greeks spanned many centuries, from about 1600 B.C.E. to 146 B.C.E. As their world was unfolding, their Mediterranean neighbors included Egypt, whose civilization had already been around 2,000 years. To the east, in modern-day Turkey, the Hittites made up another powerful kingdom that jostled with Egypt for control over Syria, which lay between them. The nearby Phoenicians first developed an alphabet and advanced the art of shipbuilding. Trade and exchanges of culture and technology flourished among these Mediterranean kingdoms, which also came to include the early Greeks.

Greece was never a unified country in antiquity. Rather, it was a collection of perhaps as many as 1,500 often fiercely independent city-states (a city that functions as a separate nation). The people of those city-states shared a culture and a language, even though they were scattered throughout the modern-day Greek mainland in southeastern Europe and around the Mediterranean and Black Seas (including today's Turkey,

North Africa, and southern Italy) like frogs around a pond, according to the Greek philosopher Plato (c. 429–c. 347 b.c.e). They did not call themselves Greeks; that comes from the Romans, who called them *Graeci.* The Greeks always referred to themselves, and still do, as *Hellenes. Hellas* was their word for the entire Greek world, and is what Greeks today call their nation.

The image that most likely comes to mind when we say "ancient Greeks" is that of Athens in the fifth century B.C.E.–what today is known as Classical Greece. Perhaps we imagine a scene from the crowded agora, or marketplace, bustling with vendors and shoppers; or philosophers such as Socrates (c. 470–399 B.C.E.), who drew crowds around them as they discussed their ideas about how to live a virtuous life; or perhaps the Parthenon, the architectural masterpiece of its day; or graceful statues of the gods and goddesses featured in Greek mythology, and the stories about them that are still told today. All of those impressions come from the era during which the Greeks were most influential, under the leadership of their largest city-state, Athens. We should also think of Classical Greece during our election campaigns, because the idea of democracy was invented by the ancient Greeks.

First Aegean Kingdom
Ruins of the Palace at Knossos in Crete (c. 1500 B.C.E.) reveal that the Minoans, who were among the ancestors of the ancient Greeks, had a highly developed society.

The Earliest Greeks

The large island of Crete, south of Greece, was home to the Minoans (who did not speak Greek), the first Aegean kingdom. By about 2000 B.C.E. Minoans were building elaborate palaces that had running water and drainage in most rooms. They had a highly developed society with a complex religion.

The Minoan culture eventually overlapped with the more aggressive Mycenaeans–named by historians for the city of Mycenae on southern Greece's Peloponnese Peninsula. Historians consider the Mycenaeans to be the first ancient Greeks, connected to the future

Greek civilization by language and religion. The Mycenaean era lasted roughly from 1600 to 1200 B.C.E., and it gave the Greeks the glorious legends of King Agamemnon and Achilles fighting at Troy, and of Odysseus traveling home from the Trojan War. The Mycenaeans, it is believed, absorbed the Minoan kingdom, and Crete later became part of the Greek Empire.

During the 12th century B.C.E., chaotic invasions disrupted the Mediterranean region. It is not known exactly what or who caused the disruption of the Mycenaean civilization, and there is a gap of several hundred years in the history of the entire Mediterranean region about which very little is known—a time some historians have referred to as a Dark Age. But by the mid-eighth century B.C.E., the descendants of the Mycenaeans had begun forming city-states around the Aegean Sea and were sending forth emigrants who spread their language and culture via new colonies around the Mediterranean.

Geography Prevents Unification

Historians question whether the Greeks could have formed a unified state with a single capital. Their geography certainly did not encourage it. Greece is a land of mountains, and the mainland is separated south from north by water, except for a narrow hinge of land, called an isthmus, near the city of Corinth. Many of the mainland's city-states hugged the coastline and were accessible only by sea, since land travel was difficult and there are no navigable rivers in Greece. Many Greeks also lived on the islands dotting the country's coasts. Each settlement therefore grew into an independent city-state with its own calendar, coins, laws, and government. They were united by a common language and religion, but they were politically divided.

The Greeks were also bound together by a shared culture—the stories of their favorite heroes and of the gods and goddesses whom they hoped would smile down upon them. In 776 B.C.E., the first all-Greek athletics competition was held in honor of their chief god, Zeus. In an event that signified their sense of unity, Greek men came together from across their varied world to Olympia in northern Greece to compete in races, wrestling, and other athletic events. The Greeks continued holding Olympic Games every four years for 10 centuries.

As another consequence of their geography, the Greeks became expert seafarers. Their comfort at sea, coupled with the sophisticated economies of their Mediterranean neighbors, led them to become international traders first and warriors second.

WHAT ARE CONNECTIONS?
Throughout this book, and all the books in the Great Empires of the Past series, you will find Connections boxes. They point out ideas, inventions, art, food, customs, and more from this empire that are still part of our world today. Nations and cultures in remote history can seem far removed from our world, but these connections demonstrate how our everyday lives have been shaped by the peoples of the past.

Athens and Sparta Become Primary Greek Powers

By about 600 B.C.E. Sparta and Athens had emerged as the dominant Greek city-states—Sparta on the Peloponnese Peninsula, Athens in the region northeast of Sparta known as Attica. Corinth and Thebes also were significant powers. The eighth, seventh, and sixth centuries B.C.E. are an era classified by historians as Archaic Greece. This is when Homer's epic stories about the Trojan War and its aftermath, *The Iliad* and *The Odyssey*, considered by the Greeks to be their own ancient Mycenaean history, were written down. Another writer, Hesiod, wrote down the oral legends about Greek gods. (The exact birth and death dates of Homer and Hesiod are not known—in fact, Homer's actual existence is not even certain—but Hesiod was active in the eighth century B.C.E. and the origins of works attributed to Homer have also been traced to that period). Sixth century B.C.E. philosopher-scientists asked questions about the universe, no longer satisfied with the explanation that the gods had arranged everything. Governments ruled by oligarchies, or aristocratic councils, were being developed among city-states. By the end of the sixth century B.C.E. there were no kings or emperors in ancient Greece, except in Sparta, and its dual kingship, a vestige of its past, had limited power.

What we call today the Classical Greek era emerged in the fifth century B.C.E. and lasted through most of the fourth century B.C.E. In the 400s B.C.E. Athens truly became the heart of Classical Greece. It was a military and cultural leader among city-states, and it also put into practice democracy, which is government by the demos, the Greek word for "people." Athens used its mighty navy to establish a maritime empire, taking control of many other city-states. Through increased contact, some Athenian notions of democracy spread around the region.

Beginning with Athenian leader Pericles (c. 495–429 B.C.E.), democracy took on its fullest form from 450 to 350 B.C.E., when Athens's male citizens enjoyed broad government participation. Women and non-citizens (which included all foreigners and slaves), however, could not participate—a situation similar to the United States until the 20th century. Greek democracy lasted in stronger or weaker forms until the Roman Republic completed its takeover of the Greek world in 146 B.C.E. It would be many more centuries before democracy appeared again in the Western world.

Although they continually warred among themselves, the Greek city-states came together to fight a powerful invader, the Persian Empire, first in 490 B.C.E. When the Persians returned 10 years later and again were beaten by the Greeks, the Athenians, who had taken the lead in the coalition that fought the Persians, felt the gods had shown them great favor by granting them victory. The resulting pride and confidence inspired them to embark on an ambitious plan to embellish their city and extend their influence.

Although they ruled different areas of the mainland, the rivalry between Sparta and Athens deepened as Athens's power and stature increased. Sparta, unique among the Greek city-states, had a social structure based on a purely military model. The two city-states shared little common ground philosophically and politically, and finally went to war with one another in 431 B.C.E. in a conflict now known as the Peloponnesian War.

Macedonian and Roman Conquest

The Peloponnesian War began between Athens and Sparta, but eventually involved almost all of Greece. It left Athens greatly weakened when it finally ended in 404 B.C.E. Seventy years later the Greeks were no match for a new superpower from the north, Macedon. Its ruler, Alexander III (also known as Alexander the Great, 356–323 B.C.E.), took control of all of Greece, defeated the Persian Empire, and then, in his continuing conquests, spread Classical Greek culture across a huge area in just a few years' time. After Alexander's death his top generals each took a piece of his empire,

CONNECTIONS >>>>>>>>>>>>>>>

Ancient Greek Words We Use Today

Many words in the English language come from ancient Greek. The English word *physics*, for example, comes from the Greek word *physis*, which means "nature." The Greek word *atomos*, meaning "indivisible," led to the English word *atom*, which refers to the smallest particle of an element.

Greek words are also at the heart of many prefixes and suffixes used in English and other European languages. For example, the prefix for the word *dinosaur* comes from the Greek word *deinos*, which means "terrifying." The suffix comes from the Greek work *sauros*, which means "lizard."

The First Marathon

When Persian troops landed at the Greek city of Marathon in 490 B.C.E., generals in Athens sent the Olympic runner Pheidippides to Sparta, seeking that city-state's help against the invaders. The Spartans, however, were holding religious ceremonies and could not send troops. When Pheidippides returned with the bad news, the Greek generals decided to attack anyway, and they won a major victory over the Persians.

Today's marathon foot race takes its name from that event in Greek history. The modern marathon is just over 26 miles, which is roughly the distance between Athens and Marathon. In the first modern Olympics, which were held in Athens in 1896, the winner of the marathon was a Greek man named Spiridon Louis.

During his famous run to Sparta, Pheidippides covered about 147 miles, and there is no historical record that he ran from Marathon to Athens. (In other versions of the ancient story, an unnamed runner, not Pheidippides, ran from Marathon to Athens after the battle to bring news of the Greek victory.) In 1983, a group of runners started a new event that covers the approximate route Pheidippides most likely took, calling the race the Spartathlon. Top runners have completed the course in less than 24 hours.

The 2004 Olympic marathon was run from Marathon to Athens.

which included the Greek world, Northern Africa, and the Near East, and they continued Greek cultural traditions by furthering and preserving the study of science, mathematics, philosophy, and history. Greek became a widely spoken language in the Western and Near Eastern world. When the Romans conquered those same regions in the mid-second century B.C.E., they, too, learned from the Greeks and built upon what they learned.

When Rome finally fell eight centuries later, the classical culture of Greece and Rome was largely forgotten in the West. But the art, science, and culture of the Greeks was preserved in great libraries by the Islamic Empire, and Islamic scholars expanded upon Greek scientific ideas at a time when Western Europe had largely lost this knowledge. Classical ideas were rediscovered and brought alive again during the European Renaissance in the late 15th century C.E. Painting and sculpture (often with Classical Greek and Roman themes) and the serious study of science, architecture, literature, and philosophy all accelerated again in Europe after a long-dormant period.

In the 18th century a new republic that called itself the United States of America borrowed an idea from a distant republic: The idea was government of, by, and for the people. Like Athens's original democracy, that of the United States was not without flaws. In its early form it still offered participation only to white male citizens who owned property, and still recognized slavery as a valid institution. In fact, the Founding Fathers of the United States preferred a more Roman model of democracy—one that gave less power to citizens with little wealth. What they did borrow from Athens were the ideals of equality before the law, the participation of

CONNECTIONS > > > > > > > > > > > > >

Power to the *Demos*

Demos is the Greek word that may have the most importance to Americans today. The idea that political power belongs to the *demos*, the people, is at the heart of the U.S. democratic political system. The word *democracy* is made up of the Greek words *demos* and *kratos*, which means "power." The American democratic system, however, is very different from the original democracy of Athens, since U.S. voters do not all gather in one place to make decisions, as Athenian citizens did. Instead, Americans rely on elected representatives to carry out their wishes, a system developed in ancient Rome.

Demos also appears as the root of several English words. *Demography,* for example, means recording and studying statistics about the population in a given area, focusing on such things as age, ethnic background, education, religion, and job status. (The word also has a Greek suffix—*graphy* comes from the Greek word *graphein*, meaning "to write.")

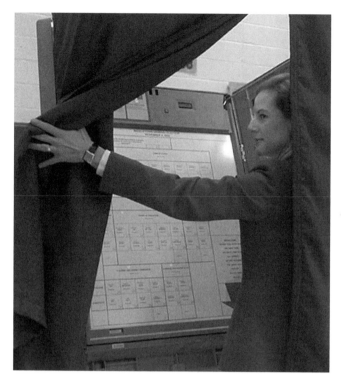

A Cherished Legacy
The idea that the ordinary people in a society have a right to help decide important issues is a concept we learned from the Greeks. Voting is one of the most obvious ways Americans today exercise this right.

citizens in their own government, and freedom of speech. In the history of the world, there have been decidedly few cultures where a playwright such as Aristophanes (c. 450–c. 386 B.C.E.) could publicly satirize the leaders he disagreed with in his plays—and win a prize for it.

To study ancient Greece one also has to examine its darker side. Slavery was universally accepted, even by the most enlightened philosophers, and meant a brutal life for many people. It was legal to abandon an unwanted baby, who would either die or be picked up by another person and raised as a slave. Women and children had few rights. War was frequent as the city-states jostled for land. While Athens could boast of the individual rights its male citizens enjoyed, it was not a benevolent leader among the city-states that it ruled.

But what set the Greeks apart from other ancient peoples were the questions they asked of themselves: How should people live? Is justice important? What values are truly worth striving for? The Greeks loved beauty and encouraged genuine intellectual and emotional inquiry and expression. The theme of all endeavors in Classical Greek art, science, mythology, philosophy, drama, and literature can be summed up in one phrase from the great philosopher Socrates: "Know thyself" (quoted in *Bartlett's Familiar Quotations*).

It is not an exaggeration to say that Classical Greek civilization is the cornerstone of Western civilization today. The Greeks left us a rich legacy, from logic to democracy to rhetoric to drama to philosophy. What emerged from their diverse city-states—from the thriving democracy of Athens to the militarism of Sparta to the oligarchy of Thrace—was a culture that set the foundation for our intellectual lives today. It is why we still study the ancient Greeks.

PART I
HISTORY

CHAPTER 1

The Beginnings of Classical Greece

HISTORIANS CONSIDER THE EARLIEST EVIDENCE OF GREEK culture to be a group that are now known as the Mycenaeans because archaeologists first found artifacts belonging to them near the ancient town of Mycenae on the Peloponnese Peninsula. Like the Classical Greeks who came after them, the Mycenaeans lived in independent kingdom-communities but shared a common language and culture.

The Mycenaean civilization began about 1600 B.C.E., though it is not clear just how it originated. Their language was Indo-European, which means it has a shared ancestry with languages from both Europe and India. Whether the Mycenaeans settled Greece thousands of years before their recorded history began, or whether they conquered people already there in about 2000 B.C.E., is not known for sure. But they are connected to the later Greeks by language and religion.

The Mycenaeans were influenced by their neighbors, the Minoans, who lived on the large island of Crete, south of the Greek mainland and not far from the northern shores of Africa. The Minoans became wealthy through their sophisticated agricultural system and trade with other Mediterranean peoples. Some of their arts and handicrafts share similarities with those of the Mycenaeans, as well.

Mycenaean chieftains or kings lived in heavily walled palaces—unlike the seemingly peaceful Minoans, whose excavated towns and palaces on Crete show no walls. An array of bronze weapons and armor has been found at Mycenaean burial sites, along with leather helmets and shields, some bronze drinking cups, and even a bronze comb with gold teeth. Weapons do not seem to have been passed down to sons and future soldiers—an indication of these ancient warriors' wealth.

OPPOSITE
Citizen Soldiers
This bronze figure (c. 510–500 B.C.E.) was once part of a vessel. It shows a hoplite with his shield–his raised arm once held a spear. Hoplites were part-time volunteer soldiers, and therefore had some influence over public policy; if they were not satisfied with their rulers, they would not fight.

By the mid-14th century B.C.E. the Mycenaeans were the most powerful force on the Aegean Sea. Warfare was rather small-scale compared to the advanced armies of the Egyptians and the Hittites, but the aggressive Mycenaeans were successful in their corner of the Mediterranean world and most likely overran and absorbed the Minoan society. The kingdom of Troy, once located along the Aegean coast in today's Turkey, was destroyed about 1230 B.C.E. While Homer wrote in the *The Iliad* of one long war between Troy and the Greeks, archaeologists think Troy probably endured several attacks over many years.

The Mycenaean towns were much more centralized than the Greek city-states that would arise in a few centuries. Everything the society produced theoretically belonged to the king, and then local rulers apportioned the wealth as they saw fit. Large palaces were built for the Mycenaean kings, and the one at Mycenae may have been that of the overall king. Striking out from densely populated towns in Greece and across the Aegean in modern-day Turkey, the Mycenaeans traveled far and wide at the peak of their civilization in the 13th century B.C.E.

The Earliest Greeks

Historians consider the Mycenaens to be the earliest Greek culture. This bronze dagger, with gold decoration is from a 16th century B.C.E. Mycenaean tomb.

Chaos Breaks Out

About 1200 B.C.E., trouble erupted all around the Mediterranean. Groups of people were on the move throughout the region, laying waste to entire cities. Palaces and artwork were destroyed, mostly by fire. Who these destructive people were remains a subject of debate. (In fact, in recent years their very existence has become a subject of debate.) In Egyptian records from the court of Ramesses III is a description, dated from around 1182 B.C.E., of attacks from "sea peoples" (as noted in Thomas R. Martin's book, *Ancient Greece: From Prehistoric to Hellenistic Times*): "All at once the people were on the move, dispersed in war. . . . No land could repulse their attacks."

The marauders caused the end of the Hittite Empire, located in eastern Asia Minor (the Hittite capital city of Hattusas was about 110 miles east of modern-day Ankara in Turkey), and the Egyptian Empire shrank back to the area along the Nile River. The Dark Age had begun.

Greek historians from the Classical age wrote that at about this time there was a large migration into the Peloponnese Peninsula of the Dorian people from the north (the ancestors of the Spartans), and that the Mycenaeans fled across the Aegean to Ionia, or Asia Minor, to escape them. Modern historians have taken their word for it, but in more recent years it has been argued that no archaeological evidence supports the idea of a large, sudden influx of invaders into Greece in that period. With improved weaponry available in the Bronze Age, one theory is that rebellious soldiers from the northern outskirts of the Mycenaean settlements sailed along the Greek coasts, where most of the Mycenaean towns were located, overthrew the leaders and spread out, looking for plunder. The Mycenaeans lost their palaces, and during the following few centuries all use of their record-keeping script ended, as did trade between regions.

The Dark Age peoples had no written language or native art traditions to replace those that had disappeared. Because people were on the move, food production around the Mediterranean world decreased. The population was drastically reduced. Except for a few pockets of prosperity, poverty became rampant throughout the region. Only Athens, protected by its location high atop a rocky outcrop, seems to have escaped large-scale destruction.

Beginning of Archaic Greece

Greeks spread out across the Aegean Sea to Asia Minor. Their

CONNECTIONS >>>>>>>>>>>>>

A Legacy in Letters

The Mycenaeans used a kind of shorthand script for record keeping that was somewhat similar to that of the Minoans. The Greeks, however, borrowed their alphabet from the Phoenicians between 800 and 750 B.C.E. The adapted the Phoenician alphabet, called *cuneiform*, to form the Greek alphabet, although they took a few of the Phoenician consonants and used them as vowels. The word *alphabet* comes from the first two letters in the Greek alphabet, *alpha* and *beta*. The letters of the Greek alphabet are still used today in Greece, even though some letters now have slightly different pronunciations.

The Greek alphabet led to the Roman alphabet, which is used today in various forms for most Western languages. Greek letters were also adapted for the Cyrillic alphabet, which appeared in Eastern Europe in the ninth century C.E. Cyrillic letters are still used today in Russia and some other Slavic countries, as well as in some Central Asian nations that were once part of the Soviet Union.

Greek letters usually appear in the West today in a scientific context. For example, the brain waves produced during sleep are called delta waves, while an active brain produces beta waves. Greek letters are also used, mostly in math. Omega, the last letter in the Greek alphabet, is written Ω and can be used in equations to refer to Ohms, a unit of electrical resistance, while Σ, sigma, stands for the summation of many variables in a math equation.

A Hero's Heel

According to Homer, the Greek hero Achilles had just one weakness, his great pride. Later, Roman writers added to the story of Achilles, saying he had a weak spot on his body—his heel. As a baby, his mother supposedly dipped him in the River Styx, which flowed through the Greek underworld of Hades. The waters protected his body from injury, but since Achilles's mother held him by his heel as she dipped him, that one spot on his body was vulnerable to attack. He died when an arrow struck his heel.

In English, the phrase *Achilles heel* refers to a person's one great weakness, either physical, mental, or moral. And the human body has a strong tissue called the Achilles tendon that connects muscles in the calf to the bone of the heel.

population had already shrunk, and no written records exist from that time. But the Greeks clung to their legends, through songs or stories told aloud, about King Agamemnon, Odysseus and Achilles, and the gods who helped them defeat the Trojans. These stories, a semihistorical memory of what Greeks believed about their past, gave the early Greeks, who were so scattered geographically, a sense of unity.

The emergence from the Dark Age coincided with the important technological development of iron tools, which improved agricultural output. Gradually, prosperity began to return. Burial sites from the ninth century, or 800s B.C.E., show increasing signs of material wealth. One Greek woman's grave dating from about 850 B.C.E. contained gold jewelry of the same design as jewelry from the Near East, which means trade had started up again. In the eighth century B.C.E. cities began to re-emerge, as Greeks and others around the Mediterranean slowly recovered from the chaos of the previous centuries. Historians refer to the period of Greek history between the end of the Dark Age and the Classical era of the 400s B.C.E. as the Archaic period, which lasted from about 750 to 500 B.C.E.

By the 700s B.C.E., one military event signaled the end of the Dark Age in many ways. A battle was fought on the large island of Euboea in the Aegean Sea between the city-states of Eretria and Chalkis. The two armies were fighting over rich farmland, and the island-city of Miletus aided Eretria, while Samos allied with Chalkis. Gone were the aristocratic officers on horseback or chariots; most of those fighting were foot soldiers. Painted pottery from that time shows soldiers with crested helmets, spears, and round shields. The battle exemplified a new era because it foreshadowed what would become life as usual for the Greeks in the next few hundred years: A Greek city-state's army of heavily-armed foot soldiers fighting with allies against another Greek city-state over farmland.

Plots of *The Iliad* and *The Odyssey*

The Iliad and *The Odyssey* are fictional epics that reflect Greek beliefs about their heroic past. The central plot device of *The Iliad*—a war between the Trojans and the Greeks—is based on real events, but *The Odyssey* is pure fiction. Both stories have become classics of Western literature, and the characters and events in them have turned up in a wide variety of books, plays, poems, and movies through the ages.

The 10-year war in *The Iliad* begins when Paris, son of Trojan king Priam, is called upon to judge a beauty contest between the goddesses Aphrodite, Hera, and Athena. All three offer Paris bribes, but Aphrodite's is the most tempting. She promises him the hand of the beautiful Helen—who is the wife of Menelaus, the Greek king. Menelaus launches an expedition to recover her, assisted by legendary warriors Achilles, Odysseus, Ajax, Nestor, and Menelaus' brother Agamemnon, king of Mycenae and commander-in-chief of the expedition. The Trojan side is led by Hector, Paris' brother.

The story recounts many conflicts within the ranks of the Trojans and the Greeks, including

Brad Pitt as Achilles in the 2004 film Troy.

actions the gods frown upon that cause the battle to tilt one way or another. Finally, the long siege is ended when Achilles kills Hector.

The Odyssey is an account of Odysseus's trip home to Ithaca. It should have been a brief trip—just across the Aegean Sea and around the southern coast of Greece—but it ended up being a 10-year journey. Along the way he and his men encountered an island inhabited by the Cyclopes, the one-eyed giant. They visited Hades, the underworld, and saw their fallen friends from the Trojan War. They put wax in their ears as they sailed past the beautiful but deadly singing of the Sirens, and farther on their ship had to sneak past a six-headed monster called the hydra.

After more adventures, only Odysseus survived to return to Ithaca. He then had to reclaim his wife and kingship after a 20-year absence. In his absence, suitors had pressed his wife, Penelope, for marriage, claiming Odysseus must be dead. But she put them off long enough to see the return of her husband, whose legendary skill with bow and arrow cleared his home of would-be kings.

In about 630 B.C.E., the residents of Thera, an island city-state, founded the colony of Cyrene in what is today Libya in northern Africa. Thera had gone through several years of drought and could no longer support its population. According to an inscription found in Thera, the emigration was declared a necessary move by the god Apollo, who was consulted through the oracle at Delphi.

The inscription makes it clear that leaving one's hometown was not always voluntary. Any man from Thera chosen to leave faced death, the inscription read, if he did not cooperate. Anyone caught hiding a chosen emigrant also faced the death penalty. If, after five years, according to the inscription, the move proved to be too difficult, colonists could return home. But the colony's efforts were fruitful and Cyrene became an important source of grain for the Greeks.

During this time Homer's poems, *The Iliad* and *The Odyssey*, which had been transmitted orally for generations, were written down in their present form, giving all Greeks, whatever their city-state, a proud past of heroes and gods, and giving Western civilization its earliest literature. Several large dialect groups emerged among the Greeks, depending on their location, but the language differences generally did not prevent communication between Greeks from different areas.

Another important writer from that time was Hesiod, whose work *Theogony* told the Greeks that their history went back to the beginnings of the universe and gave them detailed information about their gods. While some elements of those myths might have come from people who migrated to the area during the Dark Age, much of the old Mycenaean legends remained intact. Temples dedicated to the Greek gods were built at Delphi and Olympia in northern Greece and on the island of Delos.

At Olympia a temple was dedicated to Zeus, who was known as the father of gods and men, and it was here that the first athletic contests were held in Zeus's honor—the Olympic games. The first games are believed to have been held in 776 B.C.E., and athletes from all over Greece attended. The games held at Olympia were a clear indication that the Greeks, in spite of the fact that they were geographically scattered, maintained a common identity. In fact, historians tended to view the first Olympic games as the traditional starting point for ancient Greek history, until 19th-century archaeologists discovered the Mycenaeans.

Starting New Colonies

As people became more settled and prosperity slowly returned, the Greeks took their still-growing culture with them during a 200-year colonization period. Mainland Greece is about 75 percent mountains. While olives trees and grapes grow successfully in Greece's thin soil, it has few good areas for growing grains such as wheat and corn. As a city-state's population outgrew its arable (farmable) land, colonization was one solution to the potential problem of food shortages.

The first colonists were sent to Cumae in southern Italy in about 750 B.C.E. Corinth's colony at Syracuse on the island of Sicily was established in 734 B.C.E. and would become as significant as Corinth itself. Within 200 years, hundreds of Greek city-states were in place from the western end of the Mediterranean Sea in modern-day Italy, France, and Spain, to the eastern end on the island of Cyprus. There were Greek settlements on Africa's north coast, around the Black Sea, and in Asia Minor.

By sending out colonies, over-population on the mainland was relieved, additional markets for Greek goods were created, and new Greek ports were established for all the trading that occurred around the Mediterranean. Sometimes colonists went willingly, sometimes they did not.

Some colonies were founded peacefully, and wives were easily found among neighboring populations. But sometimes it was more challenging. Land had to be fought for and wives perhaps kidnapped from among the area's natives. And sometimes a colony no longer wanted a connection with the mother city. The island colony of Corcyra (modern Corfu), for example, often had a rebellious relationship with its founding city-state, Corinth.

Before any party of emigrants was sent out, the gods were consulted to make sure this was the right decision. Most often Apollo's advice was sought at Delphi, where the gods were believed to speak through priestesses, sometimes called oracles.

Sparta and Athens established relatively few colonies. Instead, they conquered the land around them. Sparta conquered a southern area of the Peloponnese called Laconia and enslaved the neighboring people of Messenia, and Athens grew into the large urban center of Attica. Sparta's only colony, in Italy, was formed to send away a large group of illegitimate males (born to women whose husbands were off at war).

City-States and Their Rulers

Greek city-states began to develop in the eighth century B.C.E. as expansions of the old villages and towns of the Mycenean era and the Dark Age. A typical city-state had an urban core, then spread out around that to

Ask the Oracle
Today you can still see many remains of the sacred buildings at Delphi. This is the Tholos temple, the gateway to Delphi. The temple, built in the early fourth century B.C.E., forms a circle, representing sacred forest groves.

CONNECTIONS >>>>>>>>>>

Welcome to the *Polis*

The Greek word for a city-state is *polis*, which is where we get our words *politics* and *metropolis*, and modern city names such as Minneapolis and Indianapolis. *Pol* is used as a suffix for foreign cities too, such as Sebastopol in Russia. *Polis* is also the source of such words as *police* and *polity*, which means a political organization.

include as much of the surrounding farmland as the city-state could control. Chances were they eventually bumped up against the outer boundaries of another city-state.

Emerging from the Dark Age, the city-states' kings gave way to councils of rulers from the cities' wealthier families, a form of government called *oligarchy* that was unusual among the ancient civilizations. Sparta was a major exception, and had two kings.

Athens was among the oldest of the *poleis*, the plural of the Greek word for city-state. It is thought that sometime in the 700s B.C.E. several villages combined to form Athens, which is a few miles from a good port, Piraeus. Originally Athens was confined to a high, flat hilltop for defensive purposes. But, like other city-states, as the population grew so did the city. Athens spread out around its hilltop, or Acropolis, which became the location for its religious buildings.

An important trade center, Athens came to control Attica, a narrow peninsula (50 miles across at the widest point) north of the Peloponnese Peninsula. Attica, with Athens as its urban core, is geographically situated for success. To its north are protective mountains, and its other sides are bounded by water (except for a sliver of land at Corinth). Because it was close to the sea, it became a not just a major trade center but a starting and receiving point for new ideas and cultural exchanges, as well.

Other significant city-states to emerge included Corinth, which was the commercial center of Greece in the 600s B.C.E. Corinth had two good ports, and its fine pottery was much demand around the Mediterranean. Thebes became a large city-state in the lush farmlands of Boeotia, the region north of Attica. Inland Sparta conquered the lower half of the Peloponnese Peninsula and was also a city-state to reckon with.

While one can talk generally of many Greek city-states that, depending on their size, shared a number of common traits, Sparta stood apart in its form of government and its social structure. Many of its customs and practices seem shocking now, but in its day it was a powerhouse that inspired not only fear but also admiration because of its devotion to discipline.

Sparta was formed when a few smaller villages combined to make a city-state. In two long wars during the eighth and seventh centuries B.C.E., ending in 630 B.C.E., this new city-state conquered and enslaved the people of a large area of the southern Peloponnese called Messenia. The Spartans were then outnumbered by their former neighbors-turned-serfs, known as *helots*, who always looked for opportunities to revolt. In response, Sparta became a strictly military society, primarily to keep watch over the large *helot* population.

The Tyrants

By the 500s B.C.E. colonization had slowed because much of the available land around the Mediterranean region after the Dark Age had been claimed. The population of Greek city-states began to increase again, as did the number of working poor. Most Greek city-states granted citizenship to all of their free-born males, but that did little to lift poorer citizens out of poverty. Farmers awaiting their harvest might borrow money or food to be repaid when their crops came in.

On the other end of the economic scale, the aristocracy, which owned the best or most land, was joined by a new class that grew rich from commerce. Some of these newly wealthy, and some members of the aristocracy who genuinely believed the social system needed reform, seized the chance to take power. These new leaders were called *tyrants*, and although today that word is used to describe a merciless ruler, it was not necessarily a negative label at first. The tyrants needed support from the city's population, especially the new type of soldiers known as hoplites.

Except for Sparta, city-states did not have professional, standing armies. All men from ages 18 to 60 (including foreigners living in the city) were expected to serve in the army as needed. The typical Greek hoplite was most likely a farmer who owned enough land–perhaps several acres that he worked alongside a couple of slaves–so that he could buy the necessary gear. The fact that the more successful Greek citizen-farmers were also soldiers, essential for defense of their city-state, gave them an increasingly powerful voice in the government. So, in a city-state such as Athens or Corinth, the successful tyrant was one who had support of the local hoplites.

In return for this support, a tyrant often helped the poorer classes by initiating large public works projects (often with wealth confiscated from the former rulers), such as city walls or new temples. Sometimes they went a step further and reformed existing laws to make the justice system more balanced.

MAKE SURE YOU ASK THE RIGHT QUESTIONS

The Greeks' oracle at Delphi, who interpreted messages from the god Apollo, was famous beyond the borders of Greece. In the sixth century B.C.E., various nations were warring over land belonging to the Medians in Anatolia, across the Aegean Sea from Greece. Both the Persian Empire under King Cyrus, and Croesus, the wealthy king of Lydia in Anatolia, wanted to expand their kingdoms. But before Croesus went up against the strong Persian forces, he traveled to Delphi to consult with the oracle.

If he attacked Persia, Croesus was told, a great kingdom would be destroyed. Confident now that he would be victorious, Croesus's army advanced against the Persians—with disastrous results. He did not gain the Median land, and he lost his own kingdom to Cyrus. The Persians, now his rulers, allowed Croesus to return to Delphi to express outrage at the advice he was given. Croesus learned that he should have asked *which* great kingdom would be destroyed.

Athens was an exception. In Athens, if the harvest was bad in a particular year, poor land-owning peasants might be forced to sell themselves into slavery to pay their debts. While other city-states managed to find ways to balance the interests of the rich and poor, in Athens the rich were reluctant to give up any of their wealth and power. Eventually, conflict between poorer classes demanding justice and the wealthy demanding payment led to threats of civil war—which, in turn, led to the most radical reform, Athenian democracy.

The Hoplites

The rise of tyrants in the bigger city-states coincided with the development of hoplites, who by the 600s B.C.E. were common in city-state armies. The hoplite soldier, outfitted with a bronze helmet and breastplate, a broad, heavy shield, and an iron-tipped spear up to 10 feet long, was extremely effective in battle. Hoplites marched in a very tight formation called a *phalanx*. Each soldier's shield overlapped that of the soldier next to him, leaving few places for enemy weapons to penetrate. The hoplites were difficult to stop as long as they stayed in formation.

Altogether the hoplite carried and wore about 60 pounds of equipment in battle, which he paid for himself. The hoplite enjoyed a higher status than the traditional soldier, who perhaps wielded just a sword, or a bow and arrows. Archers, for example, used their weapons from afar and avoided the close-up warfare the hoplites faced—because less courage was required, the archers gained less status. Archers and other light-armed soldiers were also assumed to be of a lower economic class, since presumably they could not afford the bronze hoplite armor.

In his book *The Wars of the Ancient Greeks*, author and classics scholar Victor Davis Hanson describes a likely encounter between two companies of hoplites, each representing a city-state or a confederation of city-states. The front rows of each company marched toward one another, each trying to remain in position as they broke up the formation of the other. Holding their 20-pound shields at chest height for protection, they used their spears against the enemy as the lines began to stumble or break apart. All of this was done under a blazing Mediterranean sun as the hoplites struggled in their bronze protective gear amid clouds of dust, the bodies of wounded and dead piling up around them.

Greek city-states had frequent battles with one another over boundaries or other land control issues. A city-state did not hesitate to go to war to acquire more farmland if it would mean keeping the population fed. But although war was a common fact of life, large battles between Greeks in the Archaic period were unusual. Battles tended to be brief, perhaps lasting only an afternoon, which limited casualties and better preserved the booty, since they fought on the farmland they were defending or trying to acquire.

Strict discipline was the key to a successful hoplite army, and nobody practiced discipline better than the Spartans. Sparta, unlike all the other Greek city-states (1,500 of them) developed into an entirely military state in the Archaic period. Its professional hoplite soldiers were the most formidable in Greece. In fact, Spartan discipline was so tight that the system of government remained the same over many centuries—rebellion against authority was un-Spartan.

About the same time that hoplite soldiers became a common sight on the battlefield, a new warship was being developed, called the *trireme*. Although at this time the Greeks fought primarily on land and naval warfare was rare, the trireme would prove to be a civilization-saver in the next century (see page 31).

Athens Expands Rights for Poorer Citizens

In Athens a coup (overthrow of the government) was attempted in 632 B.C.E. by a wealthy Olympic champion named Cylon. The attempt failed, but a decade later Athens seemed ripe for another violent overthrow as the ruling aristocrats squabbled among themselves. Around 620 B.C.E. they appointed Draco (dates unknown) to lead the city, with the hope that he would restore order.

The Return of the Trireme
The trireme has long fascinated naval historians and ship buffs. In 1987, Greek shipbuilders built one based on archaeological evidence of the ship's original design. And in 2004, a trireme (shown here rowing past a Greek navy vessel outside Piraeus) carried the Olympic flame to Athens for the Summer Games.

Draco's rule in Athens was so harsh—even minor offenses could result in the death penalty—that it inspired the term *draconian* to describe a merciless leader. Draco was also the first Athenian ruler to write down the laws in an official code, which meant the laws applied equally to all people, rich or poor. It also meant that after Draco's term as appointed lawgiver ended, his drastic laws remained in effect. Increasing numbers of poor farmers in rural Attica outside Athens were pitted against wealthy landowners who, in accordance with Draco's laws, were able to assume control of the property of any farmer who could not repay the money borrowed for farming or food.

As suffering among the lower classes increased and civil war seemed a possibility, Solon (c. 630–c. 560 B.C.E.) was chosen by the oligarchs to be chief lawgiver in 594 B.C.E., with the authority to institute reforms in the city's government. Solon was the logical choice for the position: He was born into the aristocratic class but was not personally wealthy, and he strove for a fairer balance between Athenian society's top and bottom layers. An intellectual and a poet, Solon restored control of confiscated land to the poor and abolished enslavement to collect debts; all peasants who had sold themselves into slavery for indebtedness were declared free. Use of the death penalty was primarily reserved for the crime of murder.

More importantly, any male citizen could use the courts to seek redress for injustices or wrongdoing, and although it did not have much real power, a council was formed to work with government officials. The idea was born that political power for a broader range of male citizens and justice for all Athenian citizens were to be matters of law. Solon, though only in power for a year, remained a revered figure among Greeks in subsequent centuries.

But in spite of his improvements and a bustling economy, poverty still prevailed. Tension among the city's poor ran high. It was time for Athens's first tyrant.

Pisistratus (d. 527 B.C.E.) was a respected army commander who seized power in 560 B.C.E. His rule over Athens was firm by 546 B.C.E. and continued until his death the next year, when his son Hippias (d. 490 B.C.E.) assumed leadership. Pisistratus left Solon's reforms in place, and further appealed to Athens's poor by instituting public works projects to provide employment. During Hippias's term one of Athens's leading families, the Alcmaeonids, appealed to Sparta for help in removing him from office. The Spartans were glad to help, and one of the Alcmaeonids, Cleisthenes

(c. 570–c. 500 B.C.E.), assumed leadership of Athens.

In the meantime, Athens continued its experiments with new government institutions. Solon's creation of a citizen council was an important early step toward democracy. It gave non-aristocratic, even poor citizens some voice in their government—if only a very faint voice. This concept was unique in the ancient world, and in the eyes of many aristocrats was synonymous with dangerous mob rule.

Cleisthenes, who was from the same aristocratic family as Solon, firmly set Athens in the direction of democracy when he came to power in 508 B.C.E. by creating an assembly of citizens with real power (see page 59).

Across the Aegean, Ionian Greeks had more than inter-city squabbles or would-be tyrants to contend with. They had become subjects of the Lydian king, Croesus (d. c. 546 B.C.E.). The newly-formed Persian Empire, founded in 550 B.C.E. by Cyrus the Elder (c. 585–c. 529 B.C.E.), absorbed Anatolia and Ionia when it defeated Croesus's army in 547 B.C.E. In the next 25 years Cyrus added Egypt and Babylonia to his empire. He was succeeded by Darius I (c. 520–486 B.C.E.), who continued to expand the empire's boundaries and got a few steps closer to mainland Greece when he subdued Thrace, a region northeast of Greece along the Aegean Sea. But the mainland of Greece remained independent.

Not long after the rule of Cleisthenes, however, Athens was faced with a challenge to provide leadership when the Persian Empire finally set its sights on Greece. At stake was the independence of all the Greek city-states.

CONNECTIONS >>>>>>>>>>>

The Spartan Tradition

Sparta had a rigidly structured society that was dedicated to warfare. The name of this Greek city-state led to the English word *spartan*, which has several meanings. It can refer to something that is plain and simple, as opposed to luxurious or fancy. People can be called spartan if they show tremendous self-discipline or deny themselves the finer things in life. High schools and colleges sometimes nickname their athletes the Spartans, reflecting the courage and skill Spartan warriors showed in battle.

CHAPTER 2

The Athenian Empire

AT THE DAWN OF THE FIFTH CENTURY B.C.E., ATHENS WAS IN position to become the leading city-state of Greece. Its busy seaport was a sign of its prosperity–Athens pulled ahead of Corinth as the biggest trade center in the region. Foreigners (primarily people from other city-states) went to Athens to share in that success, even though they could not enjoy Athenian citizenship.

Major Athenian exports included olive oil produced from olives grown in the Attic countryside. The distinctive pottery of Athens, made from the local reddish-orange clay decorated with black glaze, became a valuable export, and Athens overtook Corinth as the leading exporter of pottery. Slaves were also an important commodity in ancient commerce centers.

The Persian Wars

With mainland Greece free from foreign interference, Athens grew large enough to fend off attacks from Sparta, its primary rival, and continued its experiment with representative forms of government. This was at a time when other Greek city-states were losing their independence. The island of Sicily, home to several city-states, endured many attacks from the Phoenician city-state of Carthage, just across the Mediterranean in North Africa. To the east, Ionian Greek city-states came under the rule of the Lydians, until all of Anatolia fell to Persia's King Darius I. Darius's empire was centered in the Near East and stretched from Egypt to present-day Afghanistan.

Athens became his target early in the fifth century B.C.E. Ionian Greeks rebelled against the Persian Empire in 499 B.C.E., and Athens and Eretria sent military aid. Darius quickly regained control of Ionia, and now had a good excuse to invade mainland Greece and add it to his empire.

OPPOSITE
Elegant Architecture
This model shows the rebuilt temple complex on the Acropolis in Athens, a symbol of Athens's power and prestige during the Classical period. The main temple, the Parthenon, is 101.34 feet wide by 228.14 feet long. It was constructed of brilliant white marble, surrounded by 46 great columns, roofed with tiles, and housed a nearly 40-foot-tall statue of the goddess Athena.

It appeared to be an easy task. The Greek world was a fraction of the size of the Persian Empire. Although Darius deployed only 20,000 to 30,000 soldiers—a relatively small force—it was still more than double the number of Greeks who eventually faced them. The Persian army arrived first at Eretria on the island of Euboea in 490 B.C.E., and burned it as punishment for aiding in the Ionian revolt. From there, Marathon offered a good landing spot on the Greek mainland, because it was flat and was close to Athens. An Athenian army of 10,000 hoplites marched to the coast to meet the Persians, and was joined by 1,000 hoplites from the small city-state of Plataea. When the Persians appeared ready for battle, Athenian general Miltiades (c. 554–c. 489 B.C.E.) encouraged the Greeks to make the first move. The hoplites marched in phalanxes into the Persians's formation. Though greatly outnumbered, the Athenians maneuvered their troops to trap the Persians between a swamp and the sea. Their heavy armor protected them from Persian arrows, while the long spears did their work.

Expecting an attack on Athens to follow, the Greek army made a 20-plus-mile run from Marathon back to Athens. But the Persians turned for home. The Greek historian Herodotus (484–425 B.C.E.) reported that the Persians lost 6,400 men, while the Athenians counted 192 dead, and the Plataeans even fewer. Although those figures may be exaggerated, they demonstrate the effectiveness of hoplite warfare.

Darius planned another attack but died in 486 B.C.E., leaving his son Xerxes (c. 159–465 B.C.E.) to exact revenge. It took several more years for the Persian Empire to return, this time with 75,000 to 100,000 soldiers, but the Persians faced a more united Greece. The Greek infantry, led by Spartan king Leonidas (d. 480 B.C.E.), numbered about 70,000 hoplites and about as many light-armed troops. As Xerxes' army made its way around the Aegean Sea in 480 B.C.E., the king correctly assumed that the smaller Greek city-states would surrender without a fight. The Greeks planned to meet the Persians in force in east-central Greece at a 50-foot-wide pass called Thermopylae, squeezed between cliffs and the sea.

The Greek hoplites delayed the huge Persian army at this bottleneck for two days, until a Greek traitor showed the Persians a little-known way around the pass and the Greeks were surprised from behind. Knowing they were now beaten, Leonidas and a contingent of slightly more than 300 hoplites remained at Thermopylae while the rest of the Greek army retreated to defend city-states to the south. The Greeks, including Leonidas, fought to the last man, and are immortalized in military history for continuing to delay an army many times their number.

Expecting an attack, the Athenians abandoned their city. The Persians then destroyed it—even the temples atop the Acropolis. Then another narrow pass, this time at sea, became the undoing of the Persians. Athens had the advantage because of its large fleet of triremes, or Athenian warships. (Just before the Persians' second trip to Athens in 480 B.C.E., a rich lode of silver had been discovered at Laurium in southern Attica, which financed a fleet of several hundred triremes.) The trireme was developed about the same time the hoplite soldier became common, around 600 B.C.E., and was most likely based on ship designs of the Phoenicians, who were expert seafarers.

The boat's designers chose a long, narrow shape that could move quickly and was easily maneuverable. The ships weighed up to 2,200 pounds, and were powered by three tiers of 170 oarsmen, which is how the ship got its name—*tri* is Greek for "three." The oarsmen rowed in unison at a speed of up to 18 beats per minute. The beat of a gong or a drum was used to maintain this rhythm. The trireme was fitted with a ramming "beak"—a battering ram made of oak and reinforced with a bronze cap that protruded from the bow at water level. The rowers propelled the trireme against an enemy ship, piercing the hull.

Under the leadership of Themosticles (c. 524–459 B.C.E.), the Athenian fleet faced 400 to 500 Persian ships off the coast just north of Athens. The triremes prevailed and much of Xerxes' fleet was destroyed. The Persian ships then turned around, leaving a still-large army behind in Boeotia. The Spartans led a successful defense effort there at Plataea, while Athens continued to chase the Persian fleet. The Persians were forced home, once again defeated by an enemy they greatly underestimated.

The key to this military victory was Greek unity. Faced with the prospect of foreign domination, 31 independent Greek city-states came

A Tale of Two Kitchens

Herodotus was interested in Persian culture and history, and included several anecdotes about them in his *History of the Persian Wars*. For example, he presents a colorful contrast between the rich life of the Persian king and the simple life of the Spartan commanders. As the Spartans chased Xerxes' army out of Greece, Spartan general Pausanias came upon quite a trophy—the war tent of Xerxes' top general, full of silver and gold furnishings. The chefs were still there, too.

Pausanias ordered them to prepare a Persian feast, as well as some Spartan food, such as a murky black broth considered notoriously bad among other Greeks that included port (a fortified wine), animal blood, and vinegar. Pausanias laughed when he saw the two meals and wondered why Xerxes, when he "enjoys such fare as this, must needs come here to rob us of our penury!" (quoted in *Everyday Things In Ancient Greece* by Marjorie and C.H.B. Quennell).

together to fight a common foe—a first in their history. Even more remarkable was the cooperation between Athens and Sparta, each of which normally viewed the other as an enemy. Athens and Sparta continued their alliance long enough to expel the remaining Persians from Ionia, Anatolia, and northern Greece. Athenian leaders were now convinced of the effectiveness of trireme warfare, and proposed forming and leading a league of city-states to build an even stronger navy, because everyone in Greece assumed the Persians would eventually return. Greek historian Thucydides (d. c. 401 B.C.E.) wrote in his *History of the Peloponnesian War* that the leaders of Sparta were glad to let the Athenians take on that responsibility.

The naval alliance organized and dominated by Athens consisted of the city-states most in danger of Persian attack: those in Ionia and on the islands in the Aegean. Larger city-states contributed triremes and their crews, while smaller ones pooled their resources to provide wealth or one ship. The alliance was called the Delian League, because the money was kept at the temple of Apollo on the island of Delos (city and other treasuries often were kept at a temple where, it was believed, the god would protect them).

From League to Empire

Athens was a natural hub for the Delian League. The city had shipyards and it had masses of urban poor who needed jobs, such as rowing the ships. One trireme provided work for 170 lower-class paid oarsmen. In addition to rowers, each trireme carried about 30 soldiers—a few officers and the rest hoplites.

Over time the other city-states in the Delian League mainly contributed money to the collective military effort. The treasury of the league was moved to Athens, which now had large sums at its disposal.

The Cost of Greatness

In *The Wars of the Ancient Greeks*, Victor Davis Hanson offers figures on how much Athens had to spend to become an empire. To build, equip, and staff one trireme cost between 10,000 and 12,000 drachmas, with one drachma being a day's wage for the average working Athenian. Keeping 100 triremes afloat and manned for one month cost 1.4 million drachmas; at the height of the empire, Athens had as many as 300 triremes in its navy.

Compared to fighters on horseback, hoplites were a bargain, because a hoplite soldier spent his own money (about 200 drachmas) on his armor and equipment. The Athenian or Spartan government might expect to spend 70,000 drachmas to keep 10,000 hoplites in the field for one week. One good war horse, on the other hand, could cost several hundred or even thousands of drachmas.

At the outbreak of the Peloponnesian War, Athens and its allies had 400 triremes at their disposal. Sparta had none and its allies had 100. Sparta, as usual, preferred to invest in hoplites—it commanded 40,000 as the war began, while Athens commanded 23,000.

Even though it eventually became apparent that the Persians were not returning to Greece, military delegations from Athens were quick to visit any city-state that tried to pull out of the league. When the island city-state of Thasos, for example, tried to withdraw, Athenian warships arrived to enforce its membership.

By the 470s B.C.E. the Delian League had become an Athenian empire. Athens had built and now commanded more than 300 warships. This was a very expensive undertaking, (see the box opposite), but Athens was taking in large amounts of money from its silver mines and from the league, which had more than 150 members at its peak.

Sparta's military might protected it from Athens. Sparta had formed its own alliance, the Peloponnesian League, which kept peace on that peninsula for more than a century. Nevertheless, the growing power of Athens was alarming to Sparta.

Classical Athens

By the middle of the fifth century B.C.E., Athens saw itself as the leading city-state in Greece—and most of its neighbors agreed. The aristocrat Pericles (495–429 B.C.E.) came to power in 458 B.C.E. as one of 10 generals elected by Athens's General Assembly to be both military and civil leaders. Under his guidance the Athenian empire reached its largest size and Athenian democracy, which first budded under Solon's rule, firmly embraced many individual rights still cherished today, including freedom of speech.

Pericles made peace with the Persian Empire and also negotiated a 30-year treaty with Sparta in the 440s B.C.E. Although there was always some military action between Athens and its reluctant allies, or between Athens and Sparta's allies, such as Corinth, there were no major wars in the mid-fifth century B.C.E. and Pericles was able to lavish attention upon Athens. While the large sums of money provided by the Delian League and the Laurium silver mines was used to maintain a strong navy, Athens's income also financed some democratic reforms, such as daily pay for men chosen for jury or assembly duty, as well as a very ambitious public building program.

As Athens's prosperity continued, people from other countries and city-states flocked to the city for work. Pericles narrowed the qualifications

Great Statesman
Under Pericles, the Athenian empire reached its largest size and Athenian democracy blossomed. This bust is c. 495–429 B.C.E.

for citizenship, requiring that both parents be native Athenians—thus eliminating the possibility of marrying for citizenship. Pericles also expanded trade to the Black Sea area, from which grain and fish were imported.

With the Athenian navy employing tens of thousands of urban poor, Pericles retained his power in Athens for nearly 20 years. He and the democratic system had their enemies, though. Handing so much power over to the *demos* disturbed many aristocrats, who did not trust the judgment of the masses. Yet, in spite of some strife between the classes, life in Athens in its mid-fifth century B.C.E. golden years under Pericles was good for most people—if you were not a slave or an enemy of Athens. There was not a great economic disparity between the rich and poor. All male citizens were not only invited to participate in their own government, they were expected to. "Unlike any other community, we Athenians regard him who takes no part in these civic duties not as unambitious, but as useless," said Pericles in a speech recorded by Thucydides. "In short, I say that as a city we are the school of all Hellas" (as quoted in *The Landmark Thucydides*).

Athens's Angry Neighbors

But not "all Hellas" appreciated Athens's Classical age. Some city-states, such as Megara and Corinth, saw their trade ruined, or at least crowded out, by the expansion of Athens. Thebes, in the lush agricultural region of Boeotia, resented the power Athens held over its neighbors. Sparta to the south was becoming alarmed at Athens's growth and ambition.

Corinth, which had come to consider Athens its bitter rival, and other city-states on the Peloponnese Peninsula were under the control of Sparta, while Athens controlled lower Attica, Macedonia, and Thrace in northern Greece, the large island of Euboea, and the coastal city-states of Ionia. Much of the conflict between Sparta and Athens in the 430s B.C.E. was sparked by their tendency to meddle in the affairs of one another's allies. Sparta believed it needed to maintain strict control in order to continue dominating its large *helot* population. But Athens aided Corinth's colony, Corcyra, when it clashed with its mother city. Then one of Athens's unwilling allies, Potidaea, sought help from Corinth to rebel. Pericles may have overseen the phenomenal growth of his city, but he also put Athens on a path to war by refusing to negotiate any of these issues with Sparta.

Twenty years after Pericles came to power, Spartan leaders no longer felt they could tolerate Athens's unchecked growth. The 30-year treaty between Athens and Sparta was not even 15 years old, but war was imminent. The Greeks had united to keep the Persian Empire from grabbing control of the mainland. Now they were about to turn on each other in what would turn out to be much more than an afternoon battle over farmland. With the extensive system of allies each had developed–the Delian League and the Peloponnesian League–war between Athens and Sparta would mean war for much of Greece.

The Peloponnesian War

The Peloponnesian War began in 431 B.C.E. when Sparta attacked the Attica countryside. Although Athens faced a powerful enemy, it was surrounded by a sturdy wall, which was strengthened just after the Persian wars. Athens's port, Piraeus, was a few miles away but was also walled, as was the road between Piraeus and Athens. The whole structure became known as the long walls. The fortified road meant no enemy could starve the city by surrounding it, since Athens had access to food through shipments coming into its port, protected by the strong Athenian navy.

The war was actually fought in phases, the first one lasting from 431 to 421 B.C.E. Five times during that period Spartan forces attacked the Attica countryside, destroying crops while rural residents took refuge within the already-crowded city of Athens. Spartan soldiers stayed for just a few weeks, always fearful of leaving their *helots* unguarded for too long. But in those few weeks they ravaged the countryside, trying to draw the Attica hoplite farmers out from behind Athens's walls for a fight.

Although Attica did not have very fertile farmland, it had well-established olive groves. The Spartan attacks destroyed olive crops ready for harvest, or sometimes the trees themselves. Olive trees take at least 10 years to bear fruit, and several more years to reach their productive peak, so their destruction greatly disrupted the livelihood of Attica's farmers. In addition, conditions inside the walls of Athens, now seriously crowded with

Walled City
This modern photo shows the remnants of the strong walls that encircled ancient Athens, its port city of Piraeus, and the road that connected the two. The walls enabled Athens to hold off Spartan attacks.

refugees, encouraged the spread of disease. By the second year of the war, plague swept through the packed streets. In 429 B.C.E. the plague claimed Pericles himself, as well as many of the city's able-bodied men, who were needed to row the Athenian triremes.

Still, Athens did not send out its hoplites against those of Sparta and its ally, Thebes, both of whom had better armed and more numerous infantry. Instead, in 425 B.C.E. Athens claimed an important naval victory when Cleon, a prominent Athenian leader who died in battle in 422 B.C.E., captured the coastal Messinian city of Pylos and set large numbers of *helots* free. Athenian forces also captured nearly 300 Spartan hoplites, and told the Spartans they would all be killed if Sparta made any return visits to Attica. That kept Sparta out of Athenian territory for the remainder of this first phase of the war.

War Correspondent

Thucydides was an elected Athenian general who lost an important battle against Sparta in 424 B.C.E. and was then banished from Athens for 20 years by the Assembly. He spent that time traveling, interviewing participants or eye-witnesses to war-related events and then writing a long *History of the Peloponnesian War*—his account of the conflict between Greece's two superpowers, what led up to the war, and how it progressed in a downward spiral for Athens.

Thucydides left behind a close-up, insider's look that goes beyond the official record. He described how Athens, in the heat of war shortly after losing a battle to Sparta, committed a shameful act in the small island city-state of Melos, a former ally. The people there had tired to remain neutral, and for its lack of support Athens punished Melos by killing its men and selling its women and children into slavery.

Overall, Thucydides gave readers of history a lesson in how even a great empire can undo its own greatness. His book was not written "to win the applause of the moment," he wrote, but to serve "as a possession for all time" (as quoted in *The Landmark Thucydides*).

Athens suffered a significant loss the next year when its hoplites finally ventured out against both Theban and Spartan forces at Delium. In one day's fighting, Athens lost more than 1,000 hoplites and many of the Athenian survivors had to make a night-time run home, pursued by the enemy. Some of the Athenian hoplites (including the philosopher Socrates, whose bravery was remembered later by his pupil, Plato) continued to put up a fight as they were pursued while retreating.

In 422 B.C.E. both sides lost their top commanders: Athens's Cleon and Sparta's Brasidas. After 10 years of fighting, Sparta had made few inroads in Attica and a temporary peace began in 421 B.C.E. But there was no real end to the war. Both city-states had leaders who wanted the conflict to end with nothing less than their adversary's complete surrender.

Catastrophe in Sicily

The years 415 to 413 B.C.E. were disastrous for Athens. At the center of the catastrophe was a young aristocratic politician, Alcibiades (450–404 B.C.E.), who at one time was a member of Pericles' household. Alcibiades was one of the survivors of the battle at Delium. At the urging of Alcibiades, the Assembly agreed to send a naval force to Syracuse, one of Corinth's colonies, an ally of Sparta, and a rich and prosperous prize. Although Syracuse was 800 miles away and well-defended, Alcibiades's arguments were tempting—as were Syracuse's riches.

The expedition was approved in 415 B.C.E., and Alcibiades was named to lead it. But on the day the ships set sail, dozens of statues of Hermes were mutilated. Hermes was the god with wings on his feet who protects travelers and boundaries, among other duties. The statues had been scattered throughout the city, placed at street intersections as well as on the ships ready to set sail, and all had been damaged. The very religious Greeks would not commit such a sacrilegious act without much anger behind it. It was considered an extremely bad omen.

Alcibiades ordered the expedition to set sail anyway. His enemies accused him of the serious crime of desecrating the statues, and a ship was sent after him to bring him home to stand trial. Alcibiades defected to Sparta. The remaining ships pushed on but suffered total defeat at Syracuse, which, in addition to its own navy, had help from the new Peloponnese fleet funded by the Persian Empire. The famous Athenian fleet was destroyed and 40,000 Athenian men were killed or enslaved.

Athens was at its weakest point now since the war began, and the Spartans stationed a number of troops year-round near the city-state's walls. With Athens's defenses spread so thin, 20,000 Athenian slaves, many of them working in the Laurium silver mines on the southern tip of Attica, seized a golden opportunity and fled to the Spartans, which deprived Athens of much-needed income. Working for the Spartans now, Alcibiades went to Ionia and stirred up rebellion against Athens among her allies.

A Peace Offer Is Rejected

But Athens was not defeated yet. It had money set aside in the treasury at the Parthenon and drew on that to rebuild a fleet. It won some battles off the coast of Ionia. But within the city of Athens, a new problem arose: The ruling oligarchs were overthrown by a group of anti-democratic oligarchs who aimed to do away with the general assembly. Alcibiades, from afar, was part of the intrigue, hoping to upset the Athenian power base and return home.

Honoring Fallen Soldiers

Pericles used his very effective oratorical, or public speaking, skills to inspire the Athenians. One of his most famous a speeches was a funeral oration he gave honoring the Greek soldiers who died during the First Peloponnesian War. He also reminded the Greeks that more fighting lay ahead in what was, for them, almost a civil war.

The speech was recorded by Thucydides. After Pericles praised the accomplishments of long-dead ancestors, he said (as quoted in *The Landmark Thucydides*):

Our constitution does not copy the laws of neighboring states; we are rather a pattern to others than imitators ourselves. Its administration favors the many instead of the few; this is why it is called a democracy. . . .

Athens alone of her contemporaries is found when tested to be greater than her reputation. . . . . The admiration of the present and succeeding ages will be ours, since we have not left our power without witness, but have shown it by mighty proofs.

Modern historians have cited this speech as an important influence for Abraham Lincoln when he wrote the Gettysburg Address—a speech he gave at the dedication of a Civil War cemetery. Like Pericles, Lincoln looked back to the past as he remembered the successful American Revolution and honored the dead in a current war. And like Pericles, Lincoln talked of "unfinished work," since the war was not yet over.

Then, having received news of the overthrow, Athens's naval crews threatened to return home and restore the democratic government by force. A compromise council was formed, and it offered amnesty to anyone who had been exiled. The amnesty included Alcibiades, who in spite of his past betrayal was a highly-regarded military leader. He resumed his position as the head of a rebuilt Athenian navy and enjoyed a victory over Sparta on the Black Sea's southern coast. According to another Greek historian, Xenophon (428–354 B.C.E.), the message sent home by a Spartan officer after that battle was typically spartan in its briefness: "Ships lost. Commander dead. Men starving. Do not know what to do" (as quoted by Thomas Martin in *Ancient Greece: From Prehistoric to Hellenistic Times*).

Upon losing the battle, Sparta offered peace. But Athens rejected the offer, wanting not just peace, but to conquer Sparta. Sparta needed money to continue the war, and gave the Persians permission to re-take western Anatolia in exchange for gold. Sparta's rebuilt navy defeated Athens in battle and blocked food shipments to the Athenian port of Piraeus. Athens finally surrendered in 404 B.C.E., its days as a military power ended.

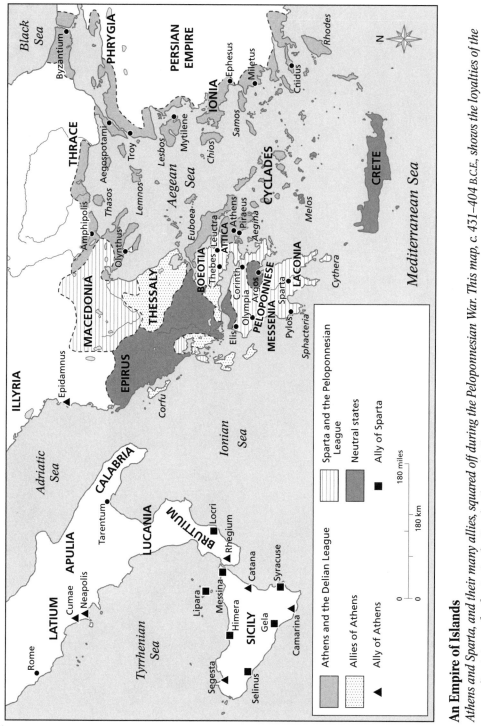

An Empire of Islands
Athens and Sparta, and their many allies, squared off during the Peloponnesian War. This map, c. 431–404 B.C.E., shows the loyalties of the many city-states and colonies in the Greek sphere of influence.

CHAPTER 3

The Final Years of Classical Greece

AT THE END OF THE PELOPONNESIAN WAR, SPARTA TORE down Athens's long walls and declared Greece free from the Delian League. Corinth pressed Sparta to completely destroy Athens, but the Spartans wanted to be sure a weaker Athens still existed as a counterbalance to Corinth. The Spartans established a new government in Athens—a group of leaders who came to be called the 30 Tyrants. This group of wealthy oligarchs reigned just eight months, but their rule was so severe (their members had no qualms about executing Athenian citizens in order to grab their property) that Thebes, Athens's long-time foe, expressed sympathy for the Athenians. Rather than see Thebes and Athens become friendly, Sparta stood quietly by while Athenians overthrew the 30 Tyrants in 403 B.C.E.

Athens went about restoring its democratic government, but the city-state did not have the finances it had enjoyed a few decades earlier. Food was scarce and the city was more crowded than ever. There was no income from the silver mines after Sparta freed the mine slaves, and golden objects in the temples were melted down to pay war debts. The Athenian empire, after a glorious half-century, was finished. Historian, M. I. Finley wrote in *The Ancient Greeks* that the devastation of Athens in the Peloponnesian War was disastrous for all of Greece, because Athens was the one city that might have been able to unify the city-states and thus maintain peace. Perhaps that could have led to a genuine nation, instead of the collection of city-states whose days of independence were nearly over.

The Rise of Philosophy

Though its status as a world power was greatly diminished after the Peloponnesian War, Athens's days of making major contributions to

OPPOSITE
Spartan Warrior
This Greek (c. 480 B.C.E.) pottery shows a Spartan soldier. The Spartans based their entire society on military service.

A Peloponnesian Peace—*Finally*

When the fighting of the Peloponnesian War ended, neither Athens nor Sparta ever recovered their former stature. The power vacuum created by their weakness made it much easier for Philip of Macedon to conquer the Greeks 70 years later. For 2,000 more years, the Greeks would be subjects of other empires, until they finally won independence again in 1829.

But the story did not end there. In 1996 the mayors of Athens and Sparta made the end of the Peloponnesian War *official* with a ceremony at Sparta. As reported in a March 12, 1996, broadcast of *All Things Considered*, the two mayors issued a joint statement that said, "Today we express our grief for the devastating war between the two cities of Ancient Greece, and declare its end." Each ancient city-state represented admirable qualities—Sparta's dedication to discipline, Athens's staunch defense of individual freedom— that, if combined today, could make a real difference in the world, the mayor of Athens told reporters.

world culture had by no means ended. Philosophy (which literally means "love of wisdom") was a sixth-century B.C.E. Ionian innovation. Philosophy means asking why and how the world exists, and what place humans have in it, rather than accepting the conventional explanation that the gods control the universe and the fate of humans.

By the fourth century B.C.E. Athens had become the international center for a number of philosophical movements. The most famous of the Greek philosophers— Socrates, Plato, and Aristotle (384–322 B.C.E.)—all became icons of new ideas and thought, and attracted many students. Socrates, executed in 399 B.C.E. (see page 106), ushered in the century and is credited with having steered philosophy toward a study of behavior and moral ethics. Socrates' devoted student, Plato, in turn taught Aristotle, who also was greatly interested in natural science and whose influence as tutor to the young prince of Macedon, later known as Alexander the Great, reached around the globe when Alexander established a vast empire.

In the fourth century B.C.E., as Greek city-states weakened and the future seemed less certain, some philosophical movements began to stress personal wisdom and inner contentment as the ideal goal for individuals. The Cynics and the Stoics were two significant movements that approached the goal of self-fulfillment from different directions. Diogenes, (c. 400–325 B.C.E.) founder of the Cynic movement (from the Greek word *kynos*, which means "dogs"), said virtue is the only true good, and that its essence lies in self-control and independence. He advocated throwing aside social conventions, which he viewed as false expressions of sentiment. A *cynic* today is someone who believes people's actions tend to be motivated by self-interest—one element of Diogenes' philosophy.

Diogenes is famous today because of a search he undertook. He supposedly walked through Athens during the day holding a lit lamp. The lamp, he said, was to help him find an honest man. Diogenes was making an ironic comment. He obviously did not need the lamp during the day, and he did really not think he would ever find a truly honest man. Today, people refer to Diogenes and his lamp when they want to highlight the difficulty of learning the truth, or when they embark on what seems to be a fruitless quest.

Zeno of Citium (c. 335–c. 263 B.C.E.) founded the Stoic school of philosophy in about 300 B.C.E. Stoics taught that true wisdom came from throwing off passions and practicing virtue, regardless of any anxiety that might result. Today, a *stoic* person is not affected by strong feelings and disregards personal comfort in order to achieve greater goals, such as wisdom and integrity.

The fifth-century B.C.E. Sophists were traveling teachers who, for a fee, gave lessons in how to use logic to win an argument. Today, the word *sophisticated* describes someone who is knowledgeable and clever. (For more about Greek philosophy, see chapter 6.)

City-States Jockey for Power

As Athenian philosophers pondered virtue and justice after the end of great conflict between Athens and Sparta, the Greek world was still finding reasons to make war—although that warfare was changing. As Athens, Sparta, and Thebes spent the next 60 years vying for the position of top *polis*, often switching alliances, Athens and Sparta had to make do with fewer farmer-citizens filling the hoplite ranks and more mercenary soldiers and armed slaves. Athens had to increase taxes to finance the ongoing wars, and Athenian farmers were finding it harder to sell their produce as other trading partners, such as Syracuse, had their own economies disrupted by war and invasions. Hence more people left their farms to join the armies as full-time professional soldiers. In fact, Greek soldiers were much in demand because they had been proven against the Persian Empire as among the best in the world.

Looking for Honesty
Greek philosopher Diogenes, shown here in an Italian Renaissance sculpture, is famous for the search he undertook, walking through Athens with a lamp looking for an honest man.

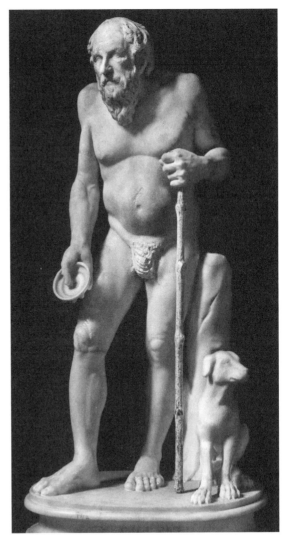

In 401 B.C.E., thousands of men joined the army of Cyrus the Younger (c. 424–401 B.C.E.), a Persian satrap (provincial governor) who was trying to wrest control of the Persian Empire from his half-brother, Artaxerxes (r. 404–c. 358 B.C.E.). One of the Greek mercenaries, Xenophon (c. 431–c. 352 B.C.E.), recounted in his book *Anabasis* how Greek mercenaries marched 1,500 miles to Babylon, were defeated by Artaxerxes, and marched another 2,000 miles back home (as recounted in Thomas Martin's *Ancient Greece*). Although the huge venture was a failure, it featured some new developments in Greek warfare that proved successful. For example, hoplites began using lighter armor and the army began making more use of men in the previously low-esteemed light-armed troops (such as archers), who protected the hoplite phalanxes at their flanks, or sides. The expedition also demonstrated that troops could travel with less baggage on long expeditions and scavenge provisions along the way. These lessons would be put to use when Alexander the Great crossed the same territory later in the century—with far more success.

In 395 B.C.E., Sparta began the Corinthian War against Corinth and its allies, Athens, Thebes, and Argos. In 394 B.C.E. it won the largest hoplite battle since Plataea in 480 B.C.E.; it was to be Sparta's last peak of power in Greece. Since Sparta's army now dominated the Greek mainland, the city-state set its sights on Greek Asia Minor, which the Persian Empire also wanted to control. Unable to take on the Persians, Sparta withdrew in 386 B.C.E., leaving rule over the Greek city-states there to the Persian Empire. Although Sparta remained the dominant force on mainland Greece, wealthy Persia checked Spartan power by financing a new fleet of ships for Athens. When a new Athenian naval league was formed, other city-states in the league, re-

Spartan Simplicity

Today, a *spartan* lifestyle means simplicity almost to the point of deprivation. The term, of course, comes from the ancient Greek people whose citizens lived in modest homes with little difference between those who were wealthy and those who were not. In fact, there was more equality between the classes in Sparta than in a large city-state like Athens because, with the enslavement of the Messenians, no Spartan citizen had to work.

Luxury and indulgence were rejected because they encouraged weakness. The Spartans also regarded cultural pursuits such as literature, art and music, as unnecessary. Xenophon wrote that the Spartans thought of food and drink as something of which "there should be neither too much or too little" (as quoted in *The Cambridge Illustrated History of Ancient Greece*). *The Columbia History of the World* quotes an unnamed visitor to Sparta as saying, upon sampling the local food, "Now I know why the Spartans do not fear death."

calling Athens's aggressive leadership of Delian League, formed coalitions designed to keep Athenian power in check. This scenario was repeated many times over the first half of the fourth century B.C.E.: Sparta or Athens would gain an upper hand until the other city-states, who may have been enemies in recent years, joined together to defeat whoever was strongest.

But Sparta, despite its military might, could never assert its leadership over fellow Greeks the way Athens had in the previous century. The city-state was unwelcoming to foreigners, and its militaristic society did not have much to offer its neighbors in the way of civics or culture. And the Spartan population had been shrinking for decades. Long years of mandatory military service meant men spent little time at home with their wives, and fewer Spartan citizens were produced with each passing decade. Sparta's army was filled with increasing numbers of non-citizens, who eventually came to greatly outnumber the Spartans themselves.

Theban Victory

In the meantime, Thebes, a growing city-state whose large population benefited from the agricultural abundance of Boeotia, unified the Boeotian territory for the first time. Its aim was defensive–centrally located in mainland Greece, it was the frequent target of invasions by other Greek city-states. Though not innovative in military tactics, Boeotian hoplites became known for their toughness in battle. In 371 B.C.E. the Boeotians, under the leadership of Theban general Epaminondas (d. 362 B.C.E.), took on Sparta. The Thebans's goal was not so much to conquer Sparta but to prevent future Spartan invasions into Boeotia, of which there had been four in just the last decade.

The generally accepted military tactic, and one the Spartans also used, was to position elite companies of soldiers on a phalanx's right side. Epaminondas modified this by putting his best hoplites on the left side of his already dense phalanx (80 hoplites across and 50 deep), to directly engage Sparta's best soldiers. The two armies met at Leuctra in Boeotia, the hoplites defended by now-common cavalry and light-armed troops who shot arrows and even flung heavy stones. Though outnumbered, the Thebans and their Boeotian allies crashed through the Spartan phalanx, killing the Spartan king Cleombrotus (d. 371 B.C.E.) and hundreds of Sparta's elite soldiers. Much to their shock, the Spartans were defeated.

The following year, Epaminondas led his army to Laconia, where a weakened Spartan army put up minimal defense. After the Boeotian army plundered the Laconian farmlands around Sparta, Epaminondas led his troops west to Messenia, where he freed the helots from three centuries of forced labor and established a strongly fortified new city for them, Messene. Epaminondas brought his army back to the Peloponnese Peninsula several more times, eventually leaving Sparta powerless beyond Laconia. Epaminondas died in a final battle against Sparta (now allied with Athens against Thebes) at Mantinea in 362 B.C.E., and Theban leadership among the Greeks faded. Though brief in its term as Greece's most powerful *polis*, Thebes, under Epaminondas, accomplished the impressive feat not only of defeating Sparta, but undoing the Spartans's social system as well, which had been based on *helot* labor.

Macedonian King
The face of this silver four-drachma coin shows Philip II, king of Macedon. It was minted in 354 B.C.E.

The Macedonians

As the Greek city-states jostled for position and power, new threats from the north were forming. Philip II of Macedon was adding other northern kingdoms to his own and had already gained territory in central Greece.

Macedon was a neighboring kingdom whose people spoke a Greek dialect and considered themselves to be of Greek ancestry. Macedon's Aegean coastline had been colonized by the Greeks in previous centuries. The Macedonians were a tough people from a rugged country whose aristocracy were constantly at war among themselves. In 359 B.C.E., ambitious 18-year-old Philip II, an able warrior, assumed power.

Philip had a year-round professional army, and the only way to pay for it was to conquer more territory. He gained a foothold into Greece in the 350s B.C.E. when the ruling aristocracy of Thessaly, the prosperous region north of Boeotia and south of Macedon, allowed Philip, whom they considered a fellow Greek, to assume command of their coalition. By the end of the 340s B.C.E., Philip had consolidated his power in north and central Greece.

The most notable leader of Athens in Philip's era was the orator Demosthenes (384–322 B.C.E.). Robbed of his inheritance by corrupt guardians after his father died, Demosthenes ended up writing court speeches to make a living. He overcame his initial awkwardness in public speaking by intensely practicing declamation (making formal speeches), and he earned lasting fame for his stirring addresses warning Athens about Philip's aggressive intentions.

Although the Macedonians considered themselves to be Greek, Hellenes such as Demosthenes regarded them as uncouth barbarians. Philip, for example, had 3,000 captured Phocians (Phocia was another kingdom north of Greece) thrown into the sea to drown. Demosthenes scorned the Macedonians as men "who always have their hands on their weapons" (as quoted in Victor Hanson's *The Wars of the Ancient Greeks*).

Demosthenes mobilized support for a Greek coalition to head off a Macedonian invasion into southern Greece, but when the Greeks allied against Philip, they faced a professional army that fought year-round. Philip took the fifth century's Greek hoplite phalanx and made it deadlier by using longer spears that weighed about 15 pounds; shields became smaller to hang from the neck or shoulders, so both hands could wield the longer spear. Philip gave the cavalry the important role of leading off the battle by charging into enemy lines. The infantry followed, aided by archers and other light-armed soldiers. And those soldiers could move quickly; they traveled light, with no entourage of servants and carrying few supplies, and they could reach any city-state on the Greek mainland within a few days.

Siege technology, used to attack walled cities, traditionally used simple ladders and battering rams. Philip's military engineers designed wheeled towers that could be rolled up to walls and complex catapults that hurled increasingly large objects to damage walls from up to 300 yards away. Philip was therefore able to conquer a walled city in a matter of weeks, whereas fifth-century B.C.E. Athens might spend months or even years trying to do so.

But despite all this technology, Philip's preferred method of taking a city was bribery—paying off city leaders in exchange for handing over the city. It was a style of warfare that had Demosthenes longing for the good old days, when there was plenty of "invading and ravaging" but "fighting was fair and open" (as quoted in *The Wars of the Ancient Greeks*).

Using both military tactics and bribery, Philip hoped to have a large empire with tax-paying members whose mines and harbors would be under his control. And his military advances proved to be extremely effective. As Hanson points out in *The Wars of the Ancient Greeks,* 30,000 Macedonian soldiers proved "far more dangerous to Greek liberty than half

MAN OF WORDS

Demosthenes is remembered as one of the great orators of Classical Greece, but his skills did not come naturally. He had a weak voice and tended to stutter, and had to work hard to overcome his defects. To strengthen his voice, he recited speeches and poems while running or going up steps. To lose his stutter, Demosthenes practiced by speaking with pebbles in his mouth. Today, these stories of how he improved his speech are well known. He is held up as a model for how a person can overcome personal shortcomings, and his speeches are still read as examples of powerful oration.

a million Persians." Demosthenes's coalition was defeated by Philip's army at Chaeronea in Boeotia in 338 B.C.E. Philip then formed a Greek-Macedonian league (which historians call the League of Corinth), and proposed that a combined army invade the Persian Empire.

With Philip II came the end of the independent Greek *polis*. Although a limited form of democracy continued in Athens, it and the other city-states would always be subject to other rulers. Within the next century the cultural capital of the Greek world would be centered in a city that had not even been founded yet—Alexandria on the Mediterranean coast of Egypt.

Great Conquerer

This statue of Alexander the Great dates from the Hellenistic Period. Alexander's extensive conquests spread Greek culture throughout much of the world.

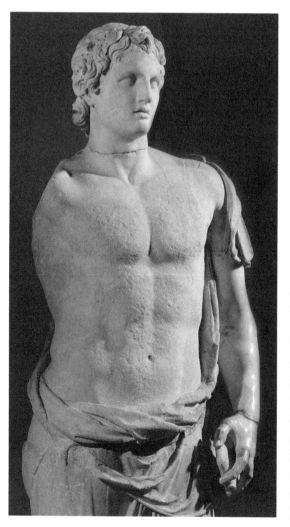

Alexander Marches on Persia

Before he could capitalize on his victory over Greece, Philip was assassinated in 336 B.C.E. Like his father, Alexander III became king at a young age but proved that youth was no obstacle to success. Alexander ruthlessly eliminated (by murder, if necessary) all rivals for leadership over the now expanded army of Macedonians and Greeks as he prepared to conquer the Persian Empire. When Thebes tried to withdraw from the League of Corinth in 335 B.C.E., Alexander's army arrived at Thebes and leveled it, except for its temples and the home of the poet Pindar (c. 520–443 B.C.E.)—whom he spared to demonstrated that he was, after all, a civilized Greek. Six thousand Thebans were murdered, and thousands more were sold into slavery. Alexander let it be known there was no turning back from the alliance for the Greek city-states.

Alexander was cruel and ruthless, and was also a brilliant military tactician. Historians tend to either admire his enormous capabilities or regard him as a megalomaniac. Always conscious of the image he projected, Alexander rode into battle at the head of his cavalry (sometimes requiring rescue by his men), his cape flowing behind him and his crested helmet polished to gleam under the sun's rays. He carried a copy of *The Iliad* on all of his campaigns. Having survived close calls with death, Alexander eventually declared himself to be a son of Zeus, the king of the Greek gods.

As Alexander fought his way through Anatolia, he claimed that his aim was to free the Greek people from Persian rule. But he actually came up against—and slaughtered—thousands of Greek mercenary soldiers. Beginning at the Granicus River in 334 B.C.E., Alexander's Macedonian-Greek army smashed all Persian opposition in Asia Minor before making his way to cities such as Tyre (in modern-day Lebanon).

By 331 B.C.E. he had conquered Egypt and founded one of the many cities named Alexandria that would dot the map of the post-Alexander world. When Alexander inflicted a huge defeat on the Persian army of Darius III (380–330 B.C.E.) at Gaugamela (in modern-day northern Iraq, near Mosul) in 331 B.C.E., he declared himself king of the Persian Empire. He needed thousands of mules and camels to haul away the huge Persian treasury of gold and other valuables.

The Hellenistic Age

Just as Alexander left much destruction in his wake, he and his successors also founded cities that spread the best features of Greek civilization and served as new markets and ports for Greece. Although he had envisioned a vast empire, Alexander did not plan for an heir. Alexander's wife Roxane gave birth to his son a few months after he died (the boy was murdered in 310 B.C.E.), but the lands he conquered were divided up among his top commanders.

Alexander's generals formed three new kingdoms that roughly encompassed the areas of his conquests. Antigonus (c. 382–301 B.C.E.) and his son Demetrius (c. 336–283 B.C.E.) became king and heir to the throne of Macedon and maintained control over Greece—which was nominally independent. Seleucus (c. 358–281 B.C.E.) took over what had been the Persian Empire. Ptolemy (c. 367–282) became king of Egypt. Their descendants would inherit these kingdoms until the Roman Empire ruled the Mediterranean world.

The city-states of Greece were no longer independent entities. Like their neighbors in other ancient civilizations, they were now part of one large kingdom. And because of Alexander, their culture became the foundation of what is today called the Hellenistic Age. (The term was coined by 19th-century historians to describe the 293 years between Alexander's death and 30 B.C.E., when the last of the Hellenistic kingdoms fell to the Roman Empire.)

Much of the wealth grabbed from the Persian Empire by Alexander was now divided up among the three kingdoms, boosting their economies and providing employment through extensive public works projects. By the third century B.C.E. the Greek language had become the common language of international relations from Egypt and Jerusalem up to the Black Sea in the north and to the border of modern-day India in the east, greatly facilitating the exchange of ideas throughout the Hellenistic world. Much like the colonial period of archaic Greece (750 to 500 B.C.E.), Greek immigrants moved to the cities in these Hellenistic kingdoms, exchanging cultural and social ideas with the local peoples.

An Invitation to Rome

Co-existing with the Hellenistic world were the increasingly powerful Romans, who by the middle of the third century B.C.E. controlled most of Italy. When Philip V (r. 221–179 B.C.E.) of Macedon tried to expand his territory into Ionia around 200 B.C.E., leaders in Pergamum, Athens, and Rhodes asked Rome to help them turn him back. Rome provided successful help, and granted the cities it aided their independence. But it was now obvious that a new power had emerged in the Mediterranean. By the middle of the second century B.C.E. Rome had conquered Macedon and most of Greece. When Corinth attempted to rebel in 146 B.C.E., it was destroyed by Rome.

Rome's power would last longer than that of Athens or the other Greek city-states, for a variety of reasons. Rome had united the other cities of Italy–something the Greek city-states had never been able to accomplish in Greece. Rome was also generous in granting civic rights to foreigners, and from this broad base of manpower could form an army large enough to conquer the Hellenistic world. And Hellenistic warfare had grown clumsy, while the Romans improved it by simplifying tactics.

Hellenistic soldiers now fought with even longer pikes, up to 20 feet long, and the once-effective tactic of using cavalry to burst through enemy lines was little used. Roman soldiers carried smaller spears that they threw at their enemy, and then moved in for close combat using the *gladius*, a double-edged steel sword (from which we get the word *gladiator*) that was much easier to handle than the long Greek spear, and which inflicted much damage. In 30 B.C.E., the last of the Hellenistic kingdoms–Egypt under Queen Cleopatra–was defeated by the Roman Empire.

PART II

SOCIETY AND CULTURE

Politics and Society in Ancient Greece

Everyday Life in Ancient Greece

Greek Art, Philosophy, and Science

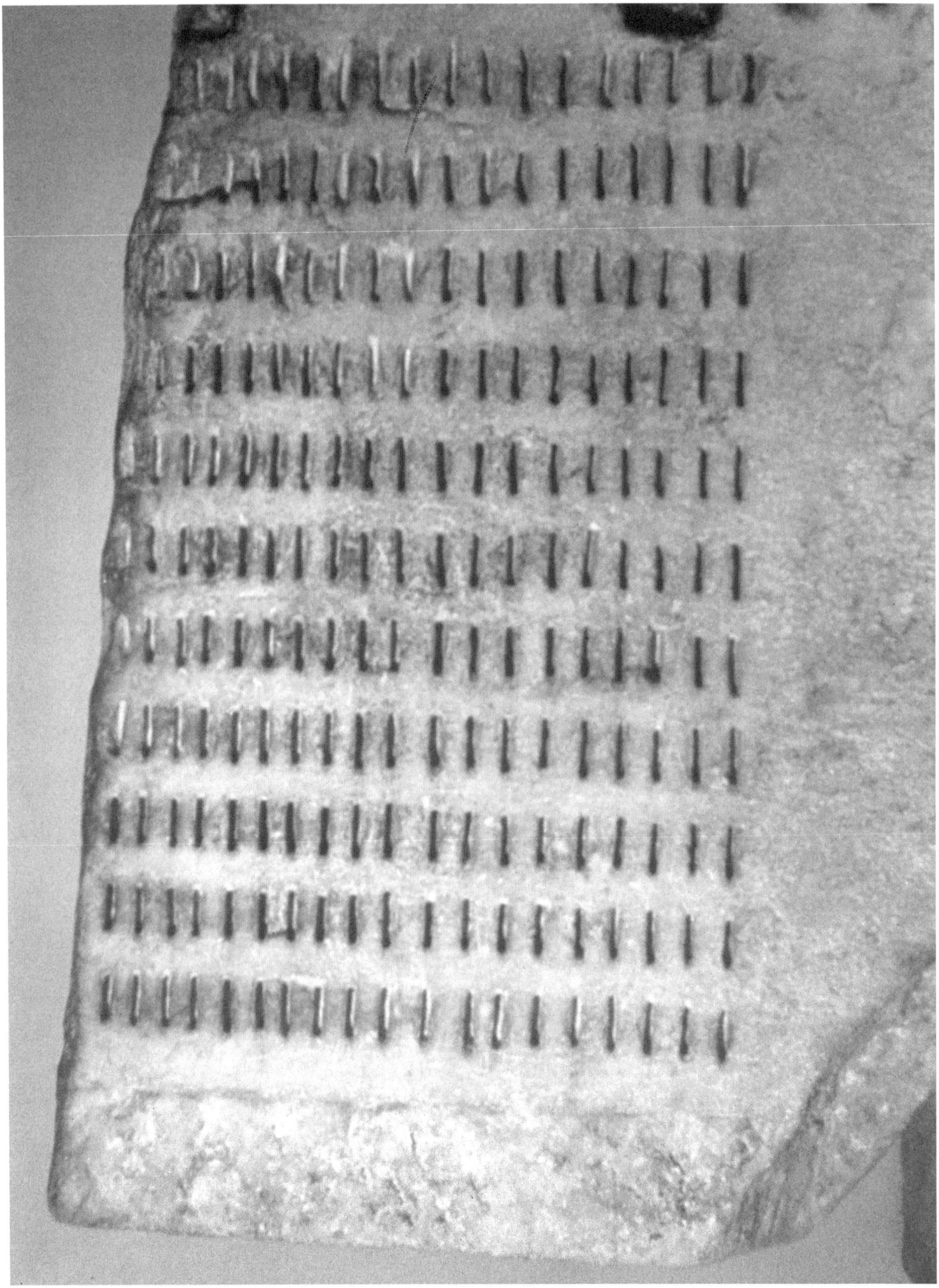

CHAPTER 4

Politics and Society In Ancient Greece

ATHENS OF THE FIFTH CENTURY B.C.E. REPRESENTS WHAT we today consider to have been best about the politics of ancient Greece. The democratic government that developed there inspired later political thinkers in Europe, North America, and other regions seeking to build free and fair societies. Yet during Athens's early history, it resisted the gradual economic and political compromises that reconciled rich and poor in other Greek city-states. The rich in Athens tried to hold on to power for too long, and the result was a radical democratic revolution in the sixth century B.C.E., as described later in this chapter.

It is important to remember that not all ancient Greeks practiced democracy as the Athenians did, and many Greek city-states never developed a democracy at all. There were always many Greeks, including some in Athens, who considered democracy to be rule by the mob—dangerous, unstable, and unwise.

Kings and Nobles

Like other ancient civilizations of the Near East, the early Greek communities were first ruled by chieftains. These monarchs led groups of families into new settlements and helped organize them militarily so they could defend themselves from outsiders. According to Aristotle in his *Politics* (as cited by John V. A. Fine in *The Ancient Greeks*), a monarch ruled with the consent of the people and had limited powers, "with the king acting as general and judge and the head of religious observances." In his role as judge, the monarch settled arguments between *oikoi*, or households.

These early Greek kingdoms were not large, usually consisting of scattered *oikoi* that relied on farming to survive. But as the chaos of the

OPPOSITE
Random Selection
The stone kleroterion *was used in Athens to randomly select a jury for a trial and to select legislative committees on which representation of all the tribes was required. Prospective jurors put a ticket into each slot in the machine, and white and black balls were dropped down through the rows. When a white ball emerged underneath a row of names, all the people in that row were selected for duty.*

CONNECTIONS >>>>>>>>>>>>

Terms of Government

The Greeks called a government ruled by aristocrats an *oligarchy*, meaning "rule by the few." The suffix of that word comes from the Greek *archein*, "to rule," and the modern English words for various kinds of government use that same suffix. Rule by one person, such as king or queen, is a *monarchy*, with the prefix *mon* coming from the Greek word for "one." In English, the Greek prefixes *a* and *an* mean "without," and *anarchy* describes a state without any formal leadership.

Dark Age ended, the population of the kingdoms grew, and the first towns grew up around the king's residence. The kings relied on the advice of the heads of the wealthiest *oikoi* to run the government. With their wealth and political influence, these advisors formed an elite class known as the *basilees*, with the king called a *basileus*. The *basilees* formed what we call the nobility. The leaders of this nobility called themselves *aristoi*, "the best," leading to the English word *aristocrat*. The Greek aristocrats looked down on what they called *hoi polloi*, "the many." That term is still used today to describe large masses of poor or powerless people.

The Rise of the *Polis*

The town where a king and his advisors lived became the heart of the political unit called the *polis*, or city. Over time, farms surrounding the city center joined the *polis*, creating a city-state, which the Greek still called *polis*. The rural *oikoi* that joined a *polis* wanted the security that came with being part of a larger community. At the same time, these farmers were used to living without direct rule, and they wanted some say in how their government was run. Assemblies, where male citizens gathered to debate public issues, were already a key part of Greek politics in the eighth century B.C.E.

As the *poleis* (plural of *polis*) developed, the *basilees* in most city-states asserted their growing political and economic strength and forced the *basileus* from power. The details of this transition are not clear, but by the seventh century B.C.E. the aristocrats as a group controlled the *poleis*, with several officials sharing the duties once held by the *basileus*. The number of government officials, or magistrates, grew as a city-state grew. Athens, for example, had many more magistrates, with specific duties, than did smaller city-states. After leaving public office, the most important magistrates sat on a council that passed laws and directed most government affairs. Council members often served for life. With the rise of the aristocracy and the councils, the assemblies—and thus the common farmers—lost some political influence for a time.

The *polis* was both a religious and a political entity, and individual city-states had a particular patron god. Athena was the patron of both Sparta and Athens, while several cities in Asia Minor had as their patron Zeus's brother Poseidon, who ruled the seas. A *polis*, the Greeks believed, would not prosper as a whole, nor its citizens as individuals, without proper homage to the various deities in charge of the universe. So a series of festivals with various rituals to please and honor the gods was built into the social fabric of the *polis*. (The religion of the ancient Greeks is explored further in chapter 5.)

Aristotle believed the *polis* reflected a natural law: Humans are political creatures and are only complete when they are living together in a community. In his *Politics* he wrote, "He who is unable to live in society, or who has no need because he is sufficient for himself, must be either a beast or a god: he is no part of a state. A social instinct is implanted in all men. . . ." (as quoted in *Ancient Thought: Plato and Aristotle*). Yet each Greek *polis* cherished its independence from its neighbors, and some developed along very different political lines. Sparta, for example, kept a rigidly ruled monarchy, with two kings who shared power, while Athens created the environment that brought about democracy, drama, comedy, and the pondering of humanity's place in the universe. Despite the achievements of Athens, however, some historians have argued that the *polis* was always destined to fail. The very independence that tolerated experimentation and encouraged diversity of thought also discouraged the tendency to work together as a united nation.

Citizens and Soldiers

Within the *poleis* were both citizens and non-citizens, who were either foreigners or slaves. Unlike most of the world before and after Greece, a person did not have to own land to become a citizen. A citizen's rights and privileges, however, varied based on social status and gender. Female citizens could not take part in politics, and only the wealthiest male citizens could hold political office. Middle-class Greeks could vote in the assemblies, but the poorest citizens could not. In their book *Ancient Greece: A Political, Social, and Cultural History*, Sarah B. Pomeroy, Stanley M. Burstein, Walter Donlan, and Jennifer Tolbert Roberts write that the history of Greece from 700 to 500 B.C.E. "is the struggle of the middle and lower classes to gain an equal share in the governance of their *poleis*." Their

THE ETHNOS

City-states did not develop everywhere in ancient Greece. Parts of the Peloponnesus Peninsula and northern Greece were dotted with small villages that lacked a central town that could serve as a political and economic capital. The Greeks called these regions the *ethne* (the plural of *ethnos*), which means "tribes" or "peoples." The residents within one ethnos shared a cultural background, but separate villages rarely took united action. Living in an *ethnos* was considered a mark of backwardness, since the people in *ethne* did not develop complex political systems.

The word *ethnos* led to the English word *ethnic* and the prefix *ethno*, which refers to a race of people or a cultural group. *Ethnocentric*, for example, describes someone who believes his or her ethnic group is better than all others. *Ethnography* is the study of human cultures.

success, however, was mixed, since some oligarchic states remained after this era. Only a few *poleis*, such as Athens, developed true democracy.

For some Greek citizens, the military was their path to greater political influence. Aristocrats were only as powerful as the *polis* they controlled, and the rulers needed strong fighting forces to defend their city or expand its influence. Most city-states relied on their citizens to also serve as soldiers, as opposed to hiring and training professional troops. Around 700 B.C.E., Greek warfare began to feature the hoplites (see page 24). These citizen-soldiers began to demand a greater say in political affairs, since they were risking their lives to defend both their own and the aristocrats' lands. The oligarchy had to give in, since they needed the military support of the middle class.

The hoplite armies led to shifts in social attitudes. Discipline was a key part of the hoplites's battlefield success. For the first time, aristocrats had to learn to work well with members of the lower classes. Middle-class soldiers showed that they could match the bravery and skill of their supposed "superiors." This battlefield experience fueled the call for greater political equality, and shaped the notion that courage in war, not noble birth, determined a man's worth to his *polis*. Soldiers fought for the honor of the *polis*, though they might win personal honor for individual heroism. Many Greeks known today for their writings and philosophy—Socrates, Sophocles, Thucydides, and Demosthenes—were also soldiers.

Changes in Athens

Modern historians know more about the political and social life of Athens than those of any other Greek *polis*. Its history offers the best example of how the average citizens gained political power, leading to a democratic state. The process of empowering citizens accelerated with Solon, a poet-politician who was given the task of trying to appease a very distressed citizenry.

Appointed as sole *archon*, or ruling aristocrat, in 594 B.C.E., Solon truly sought to defend the poor from the excesses of the rich, which included forcing debtors into slavery (see page 24). In his poem *Good Order,* Solon lamented, "The citizens themselves, through their foolish acts, are willing to destroy the great city, yielding to their desire for wealth" (as quoted in *The Classical Greek Reader*). Solon ended the practice of enslaving debtors and cancelled debts that the poor still owed. At the same time, the aristocrats would not tolerate too much erosion of their overall influence. For the most part, Solon's changes were moderate, not radical. He wanted to preserve the existing society by improving it, rather than creating something totally new.

Solon created a set of written laws that spelled out the rights and duties of Greek citizens. He divided the citizens into four distinct classes, based on wealth. At the top were aristocrats known as the *pentakosiomedimnoi*, a Greek word that means their farms produced at least 500 bushels of crops a year. These aristocrats paid higher taxes than other citizens did, but they also held the most important public offices and elected the *archons*. Be-

The Rules of Society
Solon (on the right) explains his laws to the Athenians in this 1754 engraving, based on a painting by French artist Noel Coypel (1628–1707). Solon created a set of written laws that spelled out the rights and duties of Greek citizens.

neath them were the *hippeis*, or "horsemen," whose farms produced between 300 and 499 bushels of produce a year. This upper-middle class provided most of the cavalry for the Athenian army, as well as many hoplites. They also could hold some magistracies and serve as *archons*. The next class was the *zeugitai*, which translates as "oxmen." Members of this class could afford to keep teams of oxen but not horses, and their farms produced between 200 and 299 bushels of crops a year. The *zeugitai* were usually hoplites. In government, they could hold less-important magistracies. At the bottom were farmers and laborers called *thetes*, or "poor freemen." In the military, they served as lightly armored foot soldiers or oarsmen on triremes.

The *thetes*, along with members of the other three classes, could participate in the Athenian Assembly. The Assembly, called the Ekklesia in Greek, continued to function as a forum for public debate, as it had for centuries across the Greek city-states. The Assembly also took on a new role under Solon: His legal system allowed all male citizens, rich and poor, to appeal decisions made by the *archons* and challenge the corrupt acts of magistrates. These appeals and challenges were heard in the Assembly, meaning all male citizens from every class were potential jurors. Every male citizen, not just victims of crime or their relatives, also had the right to bring someone to court for committing a crime. Prior to this, families took action against each other when the member of one family wronged the member of another family. As Sarah Pomeroy, et. al., write in *The*

Ancient Greeks, "justice was now the business of the community . . . as a whole," not just individuals or their families.

The Athenian government during Solon's time also included a council called the Aeropagus. Its members were all former *archons* and they influenced which laws were passed. Members served for life, and traditionally they came from the oldest and most powerful families in Athens. Since Solon expanded the pool of potential *archons,* drawing from the upper-middle class as well as the aristocracy, some of the old families lost political influence in the Aeropagus. Still, it normally favored the interests of the wealthy elite. The evidence is not clear, but under Solon the Assembly seems to have had some role in electing certain officials and shaping laws.

Solon's reforms also affected the economy and citizenship. He promoted the export of a key Athenian product, olive oil, while limiting the foreign sale of barley. Historians believe that grain may have been in short supply at the time, and the *polis* needed all the barley it could grow to feed its own citizens. Solon also wanted skilled foreigners to come to Athens, so he tempted them with citizenship if they and their families became permanent residents of Attica. This policy angered some Athenians, who considered citizenship a privileged status, and later rulers ended the practice.

Who Is Ostracized?

This little pottery fragment is an ostracon, *used as ballot in the Athenian practice of ostracism (see the box opposite).*

Classic Democracy

Cleisthenes, who was in power by 510 B.C.E., continued the progression toward true democracy in Athens. He wanted to break up the old tribal system, which was based on family ties within certain geographic regions (see the box on page 61). His new system split Attica into three regions, called the city, the shore, and the inland. Within each region were 10 areas called *trittys* (Greek for "thirds"). Each *trittys* included the existing towns and villages of the region, called *demes.* The number of *demes* in each *trittys* varied. Cleisthenes then created 10 new tribes, combining one *trittys* from each region to form a tribe. Citizens were now allied by their political participation in one of the new tribes, rather than by family ties. The old oligarchs could no longer count on family influence and regional power to control political events.

Cleisthenes also created a new council, called the *boule* in Greek and commonly known today as the Council of 500. Each tribe annually selected 50 male citizens by lot to sit on the council. The new council proposed issues for the Assembly to debate, met foreign diplomats, and oversaw the appointment of tax collectors.

In general, Cleisthenes's reforms expanded government involvement for Athenians. The members of the *boule* changed often, since they were selected by lot (using a *kleroterion*, see page 52), and each of the 10 tribes also elected different officials for the military. All of the reforms were approved by the Assembly, reflecting a wide level of support among the population as a whole. Herodotus, in Book Five of *The Histories*, notes that Cleisthenes was deliberately trying to win popular support, to thwart the political aspirations of his aristocratic rivals. The plan worked, because "once he had won the ordinary people over, he was far more powerful than his political opponents."

Cleisthenes's changes also set Athens on a stronger path to democracy, though government by the *demos* still faced threats, as some aristocrats considered uneducated citizens incapable of correctly using the decision-making power they were given. In the first half of the fifth century B.C.E., the Athenian general and politician Ephialtes (d. c. 460 B.C.E.), weakened the Aeropagus. The details of his reforms are unclear, but he seems to have convinced the Assembly to give some of the Aeropagus's powers to the *boule*, the courts, and the Assembly itself. Anti-democratic aristocrats then had Ephialtes assassinated, a sign of their displeasure with him and his democratic reforms. Despite this, the trend toward giving more decision-making power to the citizens of the *polis* continued, powered in part by the *demos*—the common men whose labor was needed to drive the scores of triremes that by now patrolled the Aegean Sea and the other coasts of Greece.

Periclean Democracy

During the time of Ephialtes's reform, Pericles was a major supporter of democracy, and he became the most influential Athenian leader during the Classical period of Greek history. In his *History of the Peloponnesian War*, Thucydides called Pericles "the leading man of his time among the Athenians and the most powerful both in action and in debate." He was one of 10 *strategoi*, the men elected to direct military affairs in Athens. Pericles

---

OSTRACISM

Cleisthenes seems to have introduced another new element to Athenian government—ostracism. Under this system, each year the citizens of Athens could vote to send one person out of the *polis* for 10 years. The ostracized person could then return to Athens and reclaim whatever property he had owned before leaving. This system let the Athenians banish a person they perceived to be a threat to social order. Ten years, the Greeks assumed, was long enough for a potential tyrant to lose influence in the community. Today, ostracism usually occurs within a particular social group, as its members choose to exclude or ignore someone who has upset other group members.

used his intelligence and personality to dominate Athenian politics from about 460 to 429 B.C.E.

In the government that developed under Pericles, all male citizens could participate in the Assembly after serving two years in the military. The Assembly met four times each month. Out of a possible 40,000 male citizens, 6,000 were needed to lawfully carry out a few of the Assembly's duties, such as granting citizenship to a foreigner, but other common activities could be carried out with even fewer people present. A council of educated and upper-class *archons* with the wealth and leisure time to serve in unpaid government positions still oversaw much of the government, but the Assembly's vote always ruled.

One important reform begun under Pericles was paying citizens to serve on juries. Later, people were also paid for attending the Assembly and holding some civic positions, and could eat at public expense while serving in the *boule*. These payments further opened up participation in the government, since a working man could now afford to give up a full-time job and play an active role in public affairs. When government jobs were unpaid, only the wealthy could afford to spend more than a day or two working in the government.

The Courts

The court system under Pericles also changed, though the first reforms were probably carried out by Ephialtes. These changes increased the role of the *demos* in judicial matters. All male citizens were eligible for jury duty, and a pool of 6,000 jurors was always available. Each of the 10 tribes annually chose 600 jurors by lot, picking from a group of citizens who volunteered to serve. The chosen jurors were divided into smaller groups of perhaps several hundred per trial, making bribery to influence the trial's outcome nearly impossible. The philosopher Socrates was tried by a jury of about 500, of which slightly more than half voted to convict him of rejecting the Greek religion and harming the city's youth with his teachings. He was then condemned to death. (Socrates's trial is discussed in chapter 6.)

Like the Assembly, the jury system could encompass a true cross-section of Athenian citizens, rich and poor. Under Pericles, jurors began receiving wages for the day. Trials took place in one day and each side got an opportunity to speak. Punishments for the guilty consisted of death, banishment, or a fine.

Here, as in the Assembly, the art of persuasive speaking was of much value, so sometimes a person standing trial might have a speech written for

---

PRESIDENT OF THE ASSEMBLY

The Assembly's president for the day was chosen by lot from among those present, so theoretically any one of Athens's citizens, many of whom were illiterate, had a chance to preside over the Assembly for a day. This benefit of Athenian citizenship (for males over age 20, at least) was unique in the ancient world, and indeed throughout the world for centuries to come.

While female citizens had few rights, male citizens were allowed—even expected—to attend Assembly meetings and vote on important issues. (This would be similar to American citizens being allowed to show up in the U.S. Capitol building in Washington and vote on new laws in Congress.) For example, whether or not the Athenian navy would embark on a risky venture during the Peloponnesian War in 415 B.C.E. was decided by a vote of the Assembly.

him or even read for him by someone skilled in rhetoric—the art of persuasion.

Greek Society

In general, there were three types of Greek city-state residents: citizen men, women, and children; *metics*, who could be citizens of a different city-state or from a foreign country; and slaves, who could be fellow Greeks, but were more likely war captives (men, women, and children) from another country. In *Daily Life in Greece at the Time of Pericles*, Robert Flaceliere estimates that in mid-fifth century B.C.E. Athens there were 40,000 male citizens and 20,000 male *metics*, and about 140,000 women and children citizens and *metics*. Slaves may have numbered 300,000 throughout the city-state, for a total of half a million people, of whom fewer than 10 percent had voting privileges.

Citizens enjoyed the most rights and freedoms, even the poorest-born laborers. In moving to a city-state where they would be considered a foreigner, *metics* gave up any rights to property ownership and participation in the democratic process. But in general *metics* were still valued residents, often bringing a variety of vital professional and manual skills with them. Slaves had few if any rights. More fortunate ones had some degree of freedom of movement, or lived with a family that treated them decently.

At the top of the citizen pyramid were the aristocrats, whose families had provided government and military leadership for many generations. They lived off income from land the family had held for many generations and which was worked by slaves as well as perhaps by citizens or *metic* laborers.

The civic loyalty of the upper classes of Athens made quite a difference in the quality of life for all city-state residents, because of the contributions they made to improve the city and maintain its basic functions. For example, Cimon (c. 507–409 B.C.E.), a naval hero in the war against the Persian Empire, installed a running track and shade trees for athletic Athenian men. Another wealthy man might pay for building and manning one trireme. Others paid for the religious festivals that occurred so regularly in Athens. Other aristocrats might pay for creating a public park outside the city, or for public buildings, such as the *stoa*, a covered walkway in the agora (marketplace) that offered shelter from rain or, more often in southern Greece, the hot sun. (Thomas Cahill, in *Sailing the Wine-Dark Sea*, calls the Greek *stoa* the forerunner of modern shopping malls.) The wealthiest class also paid for such mundane things as garbage removal and maintaining water supplies.

DEMES WITHIN A CITY-STATE

Athens was divided into about 140 *demes*, or villages; every Athenian resident was also a resident of a *deme*. Within the Athens city walls were five *demes*, and about a dozen more were immediately outside the walls. The rest were scattered throughout Attica. Some were quite small, with perhaps only several dozen inhabitants. The largest one was Acharnae.

Citizens and *metics* were registered in their *deme*, and the location became part of one's heredity and identity. For example, Socrates was officially known as Socrates the son of Sophroniscus of the *deme* of Alopece. Women were registered first in the *deme* of their fathers, then their husbands. Like the *polis*, a *deme* had elected officials and an assembly, and perhaps its own religious festivals.

Men of Strength

Alcaeus (six century B.C.E.) was a poet-soldier from the city of Mytilene on the island of Lesbos, one of the Greek islands on the coast of Ionia (present-day Turkey). *The Classical Greek Reader* features several of his poems that reveal a life of fighting, drinking, and enjoying the company of women. His poetry also reflects hoplite warfare and the rise of tyrants that were typical in early sixth century B.C.E. Greece. In one poem, *Walls and the City*, he wrote of the importance of "men of strength":

> Not home with beautiful roofs,
> nor walls of permanent stone,
> nor canals and piers for ships
> make the city—but men of strength.
>
> Not stone and timber, nor skill
> of carpenter—but men brave,
> who will handle sword and spear.
> With these you have city and walls.

Athens's wealthiest citizens lived in comfortable but modest homes. Athenians did not feel it was appropriate for mortals to live in mansions or palaces—that luxury was reserved for the gods. Their most outstanding architectural and artistic efforts therefore went into their religious buildings, which were considered homes for their deities; hence the beauty and magnificence of the Parthenon, which overlooked a crowded city full of haphazard buildings. In fact, any aristocrat interested in serving in the government, and dependent on the *demes* for support, knew not to flaunt his wealth. If a citizen wanted the respect of the *demes*, he spent his personal wealth on public projects.

Athens's well-educated "old money" aristocrats derived enough income from their land to live a life of leisure—they could devote time to leading the Athenian government or military without pay. In fact, the true sign of a gentleman was leisure time. Any sort of work, even something as admired as producing fine artwork or architecture, or a profession that required much study, such as that of a physician, was very much looked down upon by the upper class. A true gentleman *never* used his hands, however much intellect or skill it required (unless it was for military service or athletics).

The Manly Model of Conduct

As the society of the Dark Age gave way to a new civilization, some of the old male-oriented values remained, such as physical strength and stamina, the beauty of a muscular physique, and strong friendship among men. There was a code of excellence that all men were supposed to strive for. Odysseus, the hero of Homer's poem *The Odyssey*, was one legendary example: A farmer king, he used his strength, intelligence, and good relationship with the gods to help defeat Troy and then return home after two decades, despite many hardships and adventures along the way. His wife, Penelope, represented the ideal woman: She was beautiful and faithful to a husband who was gone for 20 years, and she continued to expertly manage their kingdom and their estate.

The Business of Ancient Greece

In addition to their other cultural contributions, the Greeks also "laid foundations of modern commerce," according to historians Marjorie Quennell and C.H.B. Quennell in their book *Everyday Things in Ancient Greece*. For affluent Greeks, land ownership remained the primary source of wealth, although the distribution of land varied from region to region. Athens, for example, had a much larger number of landowners than the lush farm country of Boeotia, where most of the land remained in the possession of a small number of aristocratic families.

Farming, not trade, was the foundation of the ancient Greek economy. Yet the Greeks were unable to grow all their own food and developed an import-export system enhanced by their skill at sea travel and by new Greek ports established by colonists around the Mediterranean. An ancient drinking cup found in Sparta (at right) is illustrated with a detailed trading scene from the Greek settlement at Cyrene on the North African coast. A ship is being loaded with a shipment of silphion, a plant similar to a carrot that was eaten and also used for medicine. The local king is watching as the cargo is weighed, then taken below deck to the ship's hold.

Greek wine, olive oil, and prized pottery were exchanged for wheat from southern Russia, fish, timber, and exotic products from the East such as spices, perfumes, and medicines. The mines of Greece, such as the silver mine in Attica and a rich source of copper at Cyprus, provided another resource for trade, while throughout the ancient world slaves

Busy Port
Arcesilas II, King of Cyrene (c. 560–550 B.C.E.), watches silphium, a medicinal plant, being weighed and loaded onto ships on this 6th-century B.C.E. Greek cup.

Spare Change
The face of this fifth-century B.C.E. silver four-drachma coin shows a bee. The practice of stamping government symbols on coins originated with the Athenians.

were always a profitable commodity. The Athenian agora held a large slave market each month in conjunction with the full moon.

Historians have speculated that the prosperity of ancient Greece, beginning in the Archaic Period, must have meant low unemployment rates, especially for those in carpentry and other building trades, and smithing, or metalworking. Many of the *metics* who flocked to Athens were unable to purchase their own homes, so some citizens became newly wealthy by renting homes to the foreigners. Renting out slaves provided another possibility for a good income for citizens and *metics*. Newly wealthy citizens often then became manufacturers or traders, while the old aristocrats would never stoop to engage in commerce.

Most men, however, had to work for a living. Among those men, farmers who owned a plot of land looked down upon craftsmen, and both of them looked down upon traders and importers, who did not actually produce anything. Working for another person instead of oneself was considered a humiliation, so all of the above looked down upon the man who had to hire himself out to someone else for a living. On the other hand, all of the above could participate in their city-state's government and legal system, which is more than the *metic*, slave, or woman citizen could do.

Greek Money

By 600 B.C.E. trade was flourishing in and out of Greek ports, both on the mainland and abroad in the Greek colonies, and the Greeks began using coins (previously, all trade was conducted using the barter system, where goods were exchanged for other goods). Herodotus credits the wealthy Lydian kingdom in Anatolia, west of Ionia the Lydians of Anatolia, with introducing coins as currency in the sixth century B.C.E., though until the Persian Wars there was little actual money circulating in Greece. The Lydian coins were made of electrum, a combination of gold and silver, and they were stamped with an official seal to prove they were genuine. When silver was discovered at Laurium, Athenian silver coins became abundant. They were stamped with an owl on one side (a symbol of Athena) and the head of a god on another. The government symbols and heads of famous people found on today's coins trace their roots to that practice.

One silver drachma was about what one skilled worker earned each day. Six thousand drachmas equaled one *talent*. An *obol* was one-sixth of a drachma, and bought enough bread for one day. One *obol* was equal to several copper coins. Each *polis* had its own coinage, and with all the money that began circulating in Greece, exchanging money and banking became common professions later in the fifth century B.C.E. It often was the work of *metics* or even slaves.

During the Peloponnesian War, Sparta helped Athenian slaves escape the silver mines, and for a while silver coins were replaced by bronze ones. Aristophanes (c. 450–c. 388 B.C.E.) has a humorous scene in one of his plays in which a character is just about to pay for some bread with his copper coins when a town crier announces that silver is now Athens's legal tender. If only he had bought the bread a few moments sooner!

Metics

By the middle of the fifth century B.C.E. there were about half as many male *metics* in Athens as male citizens. Early in the sixth century B.C.E., Solon encouraged their immigration to Athens with liberal citizenship laws, but 150 years later citizenship was considered more valuable and Pericles restricted citizenship to the children of two Athenian parents. Yet *metics* flocked to Athens, drawn by the economic opportunities they found there.

Metics had no real political power or rights, but many grew rich as manufacturers or in commerce or banking. Socrates had a friend, Cephalus from Syracuse, whose shield factory employed more than 100 slaves. Wealthy *metics*, in fact, had similar public obligations to wealthy citizens, and helped fund civic projects. Some of Athens's more notable *metics* included the doctor Hippocrates (c. 460–c. 377 B.C.E.), the historian Herodotus, and Aristotle, the great fourth-century B.C.E. philosopher.

Slavery in Greece

Slavery played a vital economic role in ancient Greece, since it provided most of the manual labor. Much like Greek citizens, the life of a slave could vary from decent to miserable. A decent life could be had if a slave worked in a home, whether town or country, where one might become almost a family member. Sometimes older male slaves accompanied sons to school with the authority to discipline the boys if necessary. And those who worked for the government or a large manufacturer who owned many slaves enjoyed as independent a life as a slave could have.

Slaves generally were foreign war captives or the wives and children of the Greeks' slain enemies. But sometimes Greeks, such as the Spartans and the Messenians, enslaved fellow Greeks following a raid or battle.

METIC OCCUPATIONS

In the years 401 and 400 B.C.E. the Athenian government awarded several *metics* citizenship for their help in overthrowing the 30 Tyrants (see page 41). The occupations listed for them included cook, carpenter, gardener, baker, household servant, and nut-seller.

Greek slaves had no legal rights and they sometimes endured abusive owners who beat them or forced them to have sex. Slaves could also be tortured to be forced to testify in legal cases. Slaves were owned by the *polis* or by individuals. Those belonging to the *polis* had more status and more freedom, often living independently. They might be put to work, for example, policing the city or cleaning up garbage, or they might be assigned to maintain the temple of the *polis's* deity.

Female slaves were often found in households or working for a merchant in the agora. Educated slaves were valuable as tutors for children in upper-class homes. Slaves often worked alongside their owners on small farms in the countryside or at crafts such as pottery, sculpting, and metal working, at which they could be as skilled as their owners. While construction of a temple called the Erechtheum was under way in the late fifth century B.C.E. Athens (see chapter 6), detailed construction records show that much of the intricate woodworking and stone carving that decorated the building was done by slaves. Hoplite soldiers would have had little strength left for fighting if not for the slaves who carried much of their equipment from place to place.

Occasionally slaves managed to improve their status. A few were able to earn money and save enough to buy their freedom. Some older slaves were freed by their masters as a reward for good service. The freed slaves were considered *metics*, which meant they could not vote and they needed special permission to own land. One rare case of a slave earning citizenship in Athens involved a man named Pasion (fourth century B.C.E.), who was freed and then managed the bank of his former owners.

The most miserable slaves in ancient Greece were either owned by Sparta, which brutalized its *helot* population, or worked in the mines. Long days in the harsh conditions of the mine made for a short life, but in general Athens did not have the problem of slave rebellions that Sparta did, since it had fewer slaves and Athenians did not treat their slaves as harshly as the Spartans did. Without slaves, Sparta might never have achieved its military strength and Athens may not have had enough silver to outfit its navy, which played such a key role in the city's rise to an empire.

Ancient civilizations, including that of the Greeks, seldom questioned the ethics of slavery. It was an accepted part of life. In fact, Aristotle argued in *Politics* that some people are naturally inferior and fit only for slavery. He said the fact that Greek slaves were usually foreigners made them barbarians, therefore inferior, therefore deserving of slavery.

Sparta, a World Unto Itself

By the time the Roman Empire controlled Greece in the second century B.C.E., Sparta was no longer a military powerhouse. Instead it had become a kind of tourist attraction, due not only to its once-legendary military prowess among the Greek city-states, but also its unique society.

The Spartans believed the god Apollo approved their form of government through the oracle at Delphi, and it was lawgiver Lycurgus whom Sparta credited with implementing it—although when Lycurgus lived or whether he actually existed is not known for sure. But by 600 B.C.E. the Spartan social system seems to have been firmly in place.

Greek tradition claimed the Spartans descended from the Dorians, the invaders who supposedly swooped down from the north at the beginning of the Dark Age. Sparta began as a few villages that grew into a city-state and eventually conquered the southern Peloponnesian area of Laconia. Sparta was the only Greek *polis* that kept a monarchy, setting up a system with two kings, perhaps as an early compromise between the larger villages. These two rulers had equal power, and one focused on wars and foreign affairs while the other dealt with domestic issues. They also served as the religious leaders of the *polis*.

The Spartan governing body consisted of the kings and a council of 28 male citizens. Collectively, the kings and the council members were called the Council of Elders. Any male over age 60 could enter the elections for the council, but most members came from the aristocracy. Sparta also had an assembly of all male citizens over the age of 30, which voted on the laws proposed by the Council of Elders. The council, however, had supreme power, as it could reject decisions made by the assembly.

The Spartan government also had five *ephors*, which means "overseers." Each year the male citizens elected new *ephors*, who supervised the kings and the council by keeping track of laws and making sure they were followed. The *ephors* provided some check on the power of the aristocracy. Sparta's laws were not written down, but were learned by children in song form and passed down orally over the generations.

NO PLACE FOR DEBATE

Unlike Athenian citizens, Spartans were not allowed to debate in their assembly. They simply voted yes or no on the laws presented to them. Spartans were expected to obey the law and not question their rulers' actions. They were said to dislike debate and rhetoric. The Spartan tendency to use simple language or seldom speak led to the English word *laconic*, which means using as few words as possible, sometimes to the point of being rude. The word *laconic* traces its roots to *Laconia*, the region of Greece that Sparta dominated.

CHAPTER 5

Everyday Life in Ancient Greece

EVERYDAY LIFE VARIED GREATLY AMONG THE ANCIENT Greeks, depending on which economic group one was born into or whether one lived in the city or the country. Within an Athenian aristocratic family, for example, a woman citizen lived more comfortably, materially, than her counterpart who sold wares at the market. Country folk in Attica dreaded leaving their peaceful farms during the Peloponnesian War to seek safety within Athens's city walls, while city dwellers might have reveled in the stimulating environment of the bustling agora. Urban life also offered greater opportunity to see various competitions during the frequent religious festivals that occurred on a much grander scale in the city than in the country *demes*.

Everyday Life in Athens

Fifth and fourth century B.C.E. Athens was dirty and crowded, and dangerous after dark. There was no organized development of the city as it began spreading out from the Acropolis at the end of the Dark Age. So after about three centuries the glorious sights atop the Acropolis looked down upon a densely packed conglomeration of little houses on narrow, winding, crowded streets.

Poorer people lived in homes made of mud brick or loosely mortared stone that were so flimsy that thieves could enter them by breaking through a wall. Some of the poorest homes were put up against the side of a rock or in small cave-like openings of a rock wall, from which two or three small rooms were fashioned. If rent was overdue, the landlord could remove the door or the roof, or block the tenant's access to water. Some Athenian dwellings were similar to modern apartment buildings,

OPPOSITE
Tuna to Go
A tuna merchant. chops the head off a fish in this red-figure vase painting from ancient Greece. Painted pottery was an important export in Athens, and is an important resource for historians today.

with several families or tenants having their own rooms in the same large building. Xenophon estimated that in his day there were about 10,000 dwellings in Athens, most of them humble.

The agora, or marketplace, was the heart of the city. Not only was commerce of every kind conducted there, but it was where mature men met to discuss politics and culture. Though poorer working women had little choice, it was considered unseemly for women to be seen there, and younger men were discouraged from visiting the agora until later in the day. Ideally, house slaves or married men did the household shopping and errands there.

Outside the city walls was the city's main cemetery. A little further west was the *deme* of Colonus and just past that was the Academy, a parklike area dedicated to Athena with a grove of 12 sacred olive trees. It was from those trees that athletic winners at the Panathenaic games received prizes of olive oil. The Academy (where Plato founded his school in 387 B.C.E.), a popular place for strolls, was also the site of a gymnasium that included a running track and a wrestling area.

Going much further out into the country was difficult, because roads were rough and only passable on foot or by donkey. In the dark, roads outside the city were dangerous, as well, because robbers could roam freely at night in isolated areas.

At Home

Most Athenians, whether in the city or the country, lived in small homes with two or three rooms. Cooking fires were usually started outside in a portable charcoal or wood stove, then brought in when the fire was hot and giving off less smoke. Fumes were vented through a small hole in the roof. The roof could also provide a quick way out for the home's occupant if, for example, a debt collector came to the door. And on hot nights people often slept outdoors on their roof.

No large or grand homes have been unearthed in Athens, though they have been found in northern Greece and on Delos. But Athens's wealthier classes did live in pleasant homes that had perhaps several rooms and an inner courtyard, and some owned both country and city houses. A house unearthed at Dystus on the large island of Euboea has two stories. On the first floor is a large hall next to the open courtyard, which may have had grapevines and fig trees. During the day the women of the household—the wife, daughters, and female servants or slaves—worked on weaving and spinning for the family's clothing, most likely in the open-

The City Walls

The first wall around the city of Athens was built in the sixth century B.C.E. during the reign of Pisistratus (d. 527 B.C.E.). After the victory over the Persians, the walls were strengthened, supposedly with the help of all the city's men, women, and children. Most residents of the *polis* lived outside the city's walls.

doored hall or the courtyard, since the weather was often warm. In the evenings the husband of the house may have entertained his friends in the hall while his wife stayed in an upstairs room. Most larger homes had women's quarters, where the female head of the household spent much of her time with her children when they were young. These quarters were often guarded by a slave to make sure no strangers entered them.

Tapestries or embroidered cloth might have decorated the walls, and furnishings were fairly simple. To dine, men reclined on couches and women sat in chairs. Each person ate from a lightweight table that could be pushed under a couch when not in use. Couches were also used as beds at night. There might also be various stools or chairs and baby- or child-sized beds.

Most people did not have a bath at home, but there were baths at the gymnasiums and the number of heated public baths in Athens increased during the fifth century B.C.E. Daily bathing or swimming in the sea was common among the Greeks. Pisistratus had fountains installed in Athens that were a source of fresh drinking water, and, when the spout was raised, for showering.

A Man's Life in the City

Wealthy Greek men of leisure had the best of what life could offer in ancient Greece: slaves to work their country property while they lived in town; wives to run their household; children to look after them in old age and ensure a fitting funeral; friends to meet at the agora, the barbershop, or the gymnasium to discuss politics or gossip; an education that enabled them to enjoy the newest literature and drama; and few social restrictions placed on their time and mobility. They had the most time to devote to politics, which was the only fitting "occupation" (though unpaid) for their status level.

Aristocratic men spent hours at the gymnasium, keeping fit between stints in the military (they were eligible until age 60). Gymnasiums also served as important social centers where men discussed politics and made business deals. A good father would arrange for his son's membership in the best gymnasium, so he would have a better chance of making influential friends. Sometimes the gymnasiums also developed into philosophical or intellectual centers, since, after all, it was where the educated elite gathered. Plato's Academy and Aristotle's Lyceum both sprang from athletic centers.

A regular outing for elite Greek males was the symposium, an evening drinking party held at one another's homes. It was a men-only

GYM SUIT

The Greek word *gymnos*, from which we get *gymnasium*, means "bare" in the sense of naked. By the Classical era, all Greek men exercised naked, their bodies rubbed with olive oil. Modern gymnasiums, or gyms, are still centers of athletic activity, though the dress code has changed considerably.

A Night at the Symposium

Scenes from a symposium were popular subjects for painted drinking cups like this one from c. 490–480 B.C.E. Athens. Here, a young man reclines on a couch while a girl dances to entertain him.

affair, although female musicians or dancers, most likely slaves, often provided entertainment. Some of these women might also carry on sexual activities with some of the men. The symposium could be a wild evening, or it could offer opportunities to socialize, philosophize, and further one's social standing. Men rarely, if ever, socialized with women in the way they did their with male friends, but one exception to that rule was Pericles' witty, intelligent mistress (*not his wife*) Aspasia (c. 470–410 B.C.E.). She often accompanied him to symposia. Today, symposia are still held, though they have evolved from private drinking parties into public events focused on discussing important issues.

Ideally, an older, married man formed a close friendship with a young, unmarried man to serve as a mentor. Sometimes this relationship was also sexual. In general, the Greeks tolerated homosexuality, at least in certain circumstances. Pederasty (a sexual relationship between an older and a younger man) was widely accepted, although in Athens young male students were somewhat protected by laws against men loitering about a school. (In the United States today, pederasty is a crime.) Pederasty was especially common, even expected, in Sparta and at times in Thebes as a way to bolster camaraderie in the military. A typical Athenian teen, as he entered manhood, would usually end his sexual relations with his mentor and get married. But some men continued to have homosexual relations while married, and two men might form a lifelong partnership.

The Lives of Women

Women were not held in high esteem in Greek society. They could not participate in, or even attend, a meeting of the Assembly. Although Greek women had far fewer rights than men, citizen women had broader rights and higher status than *metics* or slaves. A citizen woman could use the court system to address legal issues, such as property disputes, but a man had to represent her in court.

Xenophon gave future students of ancient Greece an invaluable glimpse into the role of women and how they were viewed by their male "guardians" with his *Oeconomicus*. Written as a dialogue between Socrates and his 30-year-old Athenian friend Ischomachus, the work served as a handbook for how to run a household. Ischomachus explains to the philosopher his belief that "the gods, from the very beginning, designed the nature of woman for the indoor work and concerns and the nature of man for the outdoor work" (as quoted by Sarah B. Pomeroy, et al., in *Ancient Greece*).

Ischomachus is an ideal Athenian citizen: He does not waste time with boyfriends, gambling, or other bad habits, but rather uses his time to enjoy his friends' company and involve himself in civic affairs. His wife has had the ideal upbringing: She knows should "see as little as possible, hear as little as possible, and learn as little as possible" (as Charles Freeman wrote in *The Greek Achievement*). Somewhat paradoxically, she is also a competent and educated household manager.

A Greek housewife ran all aspects of her home. She supervised slaves and servants and cared for them when they were ill. She saw to it that food was properly stored and prepared, and that the amount of food used did not exceed the amount budgeted. She was usually the family member who kept up with religious observances when necessary, and she managed the household accounts.

Ischomachus's wife learned from her mother how to weave, and just before her marriage she offered her toys to the goddess Artemis. Now she will supervise the household servants and slaves. Her indoor chores—weaving, making

Pandora's Box

The poet Hesiod wrote about the first woman, Pandora, who unleashed evil into the world. Pandora had been made by Zeus, king of the gods, and given to the Titan Epimetheus as a bride. She seemed to be an ideal woman, and had been endowed by the other gods with beauty, intellect, and musical ability. But in reality, Zeus sent her to punish Epimetheus and his brother Prometheus for stealing fire from heaven and giving it humanity.

Pandora was also given a jar that she was told to keep closed. But, overcome by curiosity, she could not resist lifting the lid. When she did, all the evils of the world escaped. She tried to quickly close the jar, but it was too late.

The myth of Pandora's jar reflects ancient Greek ideas about women and introduced a term we still use today. The Greeks believed that the gods gave Pandora and the women who followed her many qualities that would make them attractive to men. (Pandora's name means "all-gifted.") Yet women also had the potential to create evil and misery for men, especially when they disobeyed orders.

The story of Pandora is usually referred to as "Pandora's box," though the original Greek word Hesiod used meant "jar." Today, the phrase "opening a Pandora's box" means to take an action that unleashes unforeseen evils, with little hope of correcting them.

bread, folding linens—will provide her with beneficial exercise, always an important consideration for Greeks. At one point when she appears with her face covered with white lead-based makeup and wearing high-heeled shoes, Ischomachus gently informs her that he finds her natural beauty and height much more attractive. He tries to instill in her the importance and elegance of an orderly household, down to arranging pots and pans neatly and placing the vases in a good light.

The wife of a wealthy citizen spent much of her time indoors at home, though she might participate in a variety of festivals and had a prominent role in family funerals. Sometimes she visited other married women friends, or they visited her. Though her husband or a servant did the shopping at the market, she might occasionally go to a shop for something personal, such as new pair of shoes. She oversaw the rearing of her children, with the help of servants. Women who were not financially able to remain at home worked perhaps at a stall at the market or as servants.

As a girl growing up and then as a young wife, a woman passed from the guardianship of her father or another male relative to her husband. Marriages were arranged; girls were usually about 15 or 16 years old, while

The Goddesses of Greece

The social and legal inequality of women in ancient Greece presented a sharp contrast to the image of some females in Greek mythology. Zeus, a male, may have been the supreme god, but his wife, Hera, and some of his daughters—such as Artemis and Athena—also wielded great power. They could also torment men who angered them. Hera could not stop her husband's affairs with mortal women, but she did make life difficult for some of the children he produced with these mistresses. For example, she tried—but failed—to kill Zeus's son Heracles. Artemis, the goddess of hunting, sometimes attacked men who disturbed her or her followers.

The ancient Greeks also wrote about a society of women warriors called Amazons. In some stories they were said to live apart from all men. Other stories said they once fought alongside the Greeks against common enemies. In any event, some Greeks and most modern scholars considered the Amazons to be mythical. Now, however, archaeologists are conducting research that suggests a race of warrior women may have lived thousands of years ago and been the inspiration for the stories of the Amazons. Examples of warrior women have been found in Central Asia and near the Black Sea. Today, the word *amazon* is used to describe any large or warlike woman.

men were often close to 30. Sometimes fathers arranged a very young daughter's marriage years before the wedding actually took place. The primary objective in marriage, especially among the wealthy, was to produce heirs, and it was feared that women with too much freedom and too little attachment to their arranged marriages would have affairs and produce illegitimate children.

In general, the wealthier a woman was the less she was seen by people outside her family. However, most Greek families, citizen or *metic*, were not wealthy, and their female members could not afford to spend their days at home. Those women might work in the agora selling bread or perfume—citizen women alongside *metic* and slave women, none of whom enjoyed any social status.

Greek Children

Generally speaking, large families were not the norm in ancient Greece. Poorer families worried about supporting too many children, while those with money to pass on were careful not to split their estate too many ways. Hesiod advised, "Try, if you can, to have an only son to care for the family inheritance: that is the way wealth multiplies in one's halls" (as quoted in Robert Flaceliere's *Daily Life in Greece at the Time of Pericles*). A couple of centuries later, Plato similarly advised couples to have just one son and one daughter. To limit family size, women had abortions or couples left unwanted newborns outside to die or be "rescued" and perhaps raised as a slave or, if they were lucky, raised by a childless couple as their own.

Children were looked to as future providers and caretakers for their parents, and as the ones who would ensure a proper funeral for them. But the Greeks did not see children as merely an economic benefit. Judging from the number of toys that have been unearthed by archaeologists, children were more valued by ancient Greek parents than social generalizations might indicate.

A child's early years were spent at home learning about Greek culture through myths and fables. There were toys to play with: wagons or chariots on wheels that could be pulled by a string, or terra cotta dolls with jointed arms and legs. An Aristophanes play featured a character who, after spending a day serving on a jury, used his salary to buy his child a go-cart at one of the festivals that often had toys for sale. Children also kept dogs and other animals as pets.

Education with private teachers or schools was available for wealthier families' sons. Boys learned to read and write, solve math problems with

WINE FOR CHILDREN

A religious festival called the Anthesteria celebrated new wine as an entire community drank together, even children as young as three years old, who had their own little cups. Some child-size mugs have been found buried with children who died before they could participate in this festival.

Popular Toys
Engraved knucklebones like these were used in a game similar to jacks. The one at the top left says eopth, *which means "good fortune." Children also played with small wagons, dolls, and chariots.*

an abacus, play a musical instrument, and sing. Physical training for future military life was begun at about age 12 (except in Sparta, as we will discuss later). Boys also took part in sporting events at the *palaistra*, a school devoted to physical education. They practiced such sports as wrestling, boxing, and throwing the javelin.

Girls from wealthy families remained at home, rather isolated from the world, but they might receive some basic education in preparation for running their own household. Poor girls learned from their mothers or other female relatives the skills they needed to farm or manage a household. A woman's husband might also continue her education. Young girls were most visible in public at festivals. Every fourth year, for example, specially honored girls wove a new robe for the huge statue of Athena in the Parthenon. Girls might also be part of a choral performance.

Learning to read and write the Greek language was challenging, because there was no punctuation or even spaces between words. Once reading and writing were mastered, boys began memorizing poetry, especially that of Homer, which was considered essential knowledge. Poorer boys and girls would learn a trade and perhaps learn some reading or writing as a result. But most did not have the time or money to learn how to read, so oral learning, through stories, speeches, and songs, remained the way most ancient Greeks came to know about their history and current events. In general, the Athenians prized education that stressed following traditions and maintaining social order.

Country Life

The urban accomplishments of ancient Greece—the Parthenon, the theater, government, schools of philosophy—are what we remember best today. But it is estimated that as much as 80 percent of the Greek population lived outside the cities, producing the food that was consumed by city dwellers and that helped fuel the trade the Greeks had with other countries. The

Greeks knew they depended on peasant farmers for their food, so festivals were often planned to accommodate the farmers' busiest seasons.

Ploughs pulled by oxen or mules tilled the soil. Olives were harvested by climbing the trees and beating them with whip-like branches until the olives dropped off to gatherers waiting below. Wine was made by stomping on grapes inside a large basket with a spout to drain the grape juice. Fig trees provided one staple food; other staples were garlic, cabbage, onions, and lentils.

Thessaly's broad plains became known for the cattle and horses bred and grazed there. Boeotia, unlike Attica to the south, produced plentiful supplies of corn and barley. The ancient Greeks became adept terracing the hillsides to create more area to farm. Scarce water supplies and thin, rocky soil in Attica could still accommodate olives and grapes for wine. In between the rows of olive trees, Athenian farmers planted barley for their *oikos*. Athens had to import most of its grain, but this was not common among the other Greek city-states.

Goats and sheep provided milk and wool for weaving fabric, although sheep's wool was much more common for clothing. Manure was collected for fertilizer, and manure-producing animals also provided food. Bees were kept for honey.

The country farmer and his wife might work alongside two or three slaves. The farmer perhaps kept his hoplite equipment stored in his home or displayed over the hearth. The *deme* was their cultural hub, functioning like a small village, and the farmer participated in its governance as well as in the government of the *polis*.

Although agricultural life could be uncertain—droughts or crop failures pushed farmers of previous generations into slavery

CONNECTIONS >>>>>>>>>>>>>

Fables for the Ages

The plodding tortoise who defeats the over-confident hare, the wolf who dresses as a sheep to catch a tasty meal, the fox who is sure the grapes he cannot reach must be sour—these well-known stories and countless others trace their roots to ancient Greece and a writer named Aesop. Each fable has a moral—a short saying that sums up the point of the story and offers advice for readers to follow.

Some historians think Aesop was a legendary figure of the sixth century B.C.E., not a real author, and the stories credited to him were actually folk tales told orally for generations. Other sources say he was a freed slave from Thrace who may have originally come from North Africa. Some of Aesop's fables were written down around the third century B.C.E., and Roman writers began translating them into Latin during the first century C.E. In modern times, Aesop's fables have appeared in picture books and been turned into cartoons.

before Solon's reforms in the early sixth century B.C.E. (see page 24)–it was often idealized as the best way to live. Aristophanes, whose plays urged peace during the Peloponnesian War, wrote of a farmer who fled behind the Athenian walls for safety, but "gaze[d] out towards the country, yearning for peace, sick of the town, missing my own village. . . ." (quoted by Robert Flaceliere in *Daily Life in Greece at the Time of Pericles*).

Spartan Society

Spartan society changed considerably after the two Messenian Wars of the late 700s and the mid-600s B.C.E. The wars left the Messenian people completely enslaved by Sparta. No longer would any Spartan male citizen farm his own land or manufacture any item for sale or trade. From the 600s B.C.E. on, the Spartans' Messenian serfs, the *helots*, farmed their own and Spartan land and had to hand over most of the food they produced to the Spartans. Outnumbered by their very hostile *helots*, who rebelled at almost any chance (often with help from Sparta's enemies), Sparta became a strictly military society to keep the *helots* in check and to expand its power in the Peloponnese Peninsula. Confident in the capabilities of its military, Sparta, unlike most ancient cities, had no walls around it.

Under the social system that developed after the defeat of the Messenians, Spartan male citizens were prohibited by law to perform any type of work except warfare, and female citizens could only raise future hoplites or future mothers of future hoplites. All contributions from Sparta to the literature and art of Greece ceased. Individuality was almost completely subdued. Both simple and crucial decisions–from what hair style to wear to when to get married–were decided by the state.

There was little obvious show of wealth among Spartan citizens. Each citizen husband and wife received similar amounts of food, with financial equality among all citizens being the ideal. In reality, however, incomes and wealth did vary within Spartan society, and Aristotle wrote in his *Politics* that poor *ephors* were likely targets for bribery.

In general, Sparta did not welcome foreigners, although it allowed various neighboring peoples, called *perioikoi*, their independence but required them to pay taxes and fight in the Spartan army. The *perioikoi* also performed much of the commercial work forbidden to Spartan citizens.

Spartan women enjoyed considerably more freedom than other ancient Greek women. Spartan men spent little time at home, so wives and daughters did not have to attend to their needs. In addition, *helots* did all manual labor in homes and in the fields, male children left the home at age seven, and female children had freedom to play outdoors. Taken together, these factors meant Spartan women did not have many demands on their time. They could also own property, which most Greek women could not, except in rare circumstances. Spartan women freely exercised outdoors—without clothes, which shocked other Greeks—and had a reputation for talking back to their husbands and male relatives.

Spartan children belonged to the state, and boys left home at age seven to live in all-male barracks and begin their training as future hoplites and citizens—one and the same in Sparta. The Spartans placed much less value on knowledge of literature and music, unless it was for military purposes. Instead, they concentrated on teaching discipline, loyalty, and endurance. Unlike sheltered Athenian girls, who rarely left their homes, Spartan girls played outdoors, running, wrestling, and wearing very little clothing, like the boys. The idea was to raise strong young women who would bear healthy sons.

By age 12, Spartan boys had learned to march in bare feet. They were given little to eat so they would learn resourcefulness, including how to steal food. They also learned how to kill. By this age boys also were introduced to an older male lover who also served as a tutor and mentor.

Food and Clothing

Most Greeks ate simply. Meat was usually eaten only at festivals, after a sacrifice. Bread was the main part of every meal. In general, there were two types of bread available at the market: *maza* was made from roasted barley meal kneaded with honey and water or oil and cooked over heat; *artos* was a round wheat loaf baked in an oven. *Maza* was less expensive and so was more common among poorer residents. Everything else accompanying the bread was referred to as *opson*, whether vegetables, olives, eggs, or meat. Vegetables were more expensive than lentils, so lentils were another staple for the poor. Lentil soup made an inexpensive but filling meal.

A typical Athenian breakfast (one of perhaps two daily meals) was *maza* or *artos* soaked in diluted wine with a few olives or figs. (Wine diluted with water was a regular part of the Athenian diet.) People in the country had more meat in their diet, while city dwellers ate more fish, imported from the Black Sea. A favorite dish among the Spartans was a broth that included wine, animal blood, and vinegar. There were jokes about the big appetites of Boeotians, who lived in a land of agricultural plenty.

Women (or their servants) wove the cloth for the family's clothing, which for women consisted of a long dress called a *chiton* made from a

A SHINE FOR SHOES

A third century B.C.E. short play by writer Herodas (dates unknown) features two women at a shoe shop arguing with the cobbler over the price of his shoes. He rattles off his fine selection: "espadrilles, mules, slippers, Ionian bootees, party overshoes, high button-boots . . . Argos sandals, scarlet pumps. . . . " (quoted in Robert Flaceliere's *Daily Life in Greece at the Time of Pericles*).

The Importance of Olives

The first harvest from an olive tree represents a long-awaited investment: It takes about a dozen years before a first crop is produced, and another 25 before the tree is fully mature. But then an olive tree can last for centuries.

Olive oil was used by the Greeks to light their lamps, for lubrication, and even on their bodies: Athletes rubbed it on themselves before exercising, since they competed naked. Afterward, they used a tool called a *strigil* to scrape off excess oil and dirt before bathing. Greek doctors also used olive oil as a medicine to heal wounds and treat such ailments as nausea and insomnia.

The philosopher Democritus (c. 470–c. 380 B.C.E.) believed that eating olive oil led to a long life. Modern doctors tend to agree. Olive oil has no cholesterol and is one component of the Mediterranean Diet, which also includes vegetables and whole grains. This diet can lower the chances of developing heart disease and cancer, according to a study of more than 20,000 adults in modern-day Greece (as reported in the *New England Journal of Medicine*).

The olive was so important to the ancient Greeks that they passed laws limiting how many trees could be cut down each year in a grove. Modern olive farming, however, does not have similar restrictions. Today, olives remain one of Greece's most important crops, and almost 15 percent of its farmland is devoted to them. The European Union encourages farmers in Greece and several other Mediterranean countries to produce as many olives as possible, and the olives and their oil are then sold outside Europe. This lucrative trade has led farmers to abandon the old practice of spacing trees fairly wide apart. Ancient olive groves have been plowed under and new farms, with tightly packed trees, have replaced them. In 2001, the WWF (formerly the World Wildlife Fund) reported that the changes in olive farming were destroying the soil in parts of southern Europe, as well as depriving some animals of their natural habitat.

large piece of fabric, about 6 feet wide by 11 feet long. The Doric-style *chiton* was actually two dress lengths fastened with brooches at the shoulders; it hung in folds and was belted around the waist. The Ionian style *chiton* had holes cut for the arms and neck and also hung in folds. The fabric was made from finely woven wool, linen, or cotton muslin. Corinth exported ready-made robes of fine linen.

For warmth women (and men) wore a shawl-like *himation*, which was artfully draped over the shoulders, and also wore caps or veils and carried parasols to protect them from the sun. Women wore their long hair up, or sometimes curled, and decorated it with combs made from bone, ivory wood, bronze, or tortoise shell.

Men wore a short tunic, with white fabric signifying wealth while others wore natural-colored wool. Spartan children and some poorer Athenians might wear a *himation* alone, just large enough to wrap around the body. Decorated vases show people of all classes in bare feet, although there were cobblers who made shoes. Travelers often wore boots, and wealthy women wore fancy shoes.

Family Rituals

Religion played an important role in family events. Weddings often occurred in Gamelion, the month considered sacred to Hera, the goddess who oversaw marriage. (Gamelion is roughly equivalent to our January. The Athenian calendar had 10 months of 35 or 36 days each.) The evening before a teen-aged bride left to go to her new husband's home, her family offered sacrifices to several gods, including Zeus, Hera, and Apollo. The bride gave up her childhood toys, such as her dolls, as offerings, and then took a ritual bath in water from a special fountain. Her groom also took a ritual bath.

On the wedding day the homes of both the bride and groom were decorated with olive and laurel leaf garlands. The bride's father hosted a sacrifice and a banquet at which men and women sat separately. The bride was present but veiled, dressed in her best clothing and wearing a wreath on her head. Included in the wedding feast were sesame cakes to ensure fertility, and after the meal the bride received her gifts, which often included jewels. At the end of the day, a procession formed to accompany the bride to her new home. Spartan brides were carried off as if they were being abducted.

Greek marriages, especially among the wealthy, were primarily a

Greek Fashion
The women are gathering on this fifth-century B.C.E. Greek cup. They are wearing the chiton *and the* himation.

social institution with the purpose of producing children as caretakers for their parents in later years and then as heirs to family property. Aristotle was happily married to a friend's niece, and wrote of the benefits of a good marriage, but in many cases wives and husbands had little to do with each other once two or three children were born.

In Sparta, where men spent little time at home (they continued to dine with the other men in their communal mess halls even after marriage), marriage was mandatory. Divorce was legal among the ancient Greeks, but a woman could not set up her own household. She would have to return to the legal protection of a male relative if she wanted to leave her husband.

When a baby was born, an olive branch was hung on the family's front door to announce a boy, or a piece of woolen cloth for a girl. Several days after a child's birth a ceremony took place to welcome the child into the family and purify the mother and those who had attended her in childbirth. Purification rites were mandatory after a birth, to cleanse those involved from the "contamination" of childbirth. On the 10th day after a child was born, a banquet was held and the child received a name and gifts.

In Sparta, babies were considered state property. All newborns were shown to local elders—men with some degree of social authority. According to the Roman historian Plutarch (c. 46–c. 120 C.E.), the elders examined the baby. If he or she was "well-formed and lusty they allowed it to be reared, but if it was sickly or misshapen they had it taken to the place called Apothetai, a high cliff . . ." where it was abandoned (as quoted in Robert Flaceliere's *Daily Life in Greece at the Time of Pericles*). Unlike other babies of that era, who were wrapped in tight swaddling that restricted their movement, Spartan babies were loosely covered; they began their life of exercise immediately.

Most Greeks believed that after they died, their spirits, or shades, descended into the underworld of Hades, where they wandered aimlessly, experiencing neither pleasure nor pain. Certain religious cults, however, did talk about an afterlife where souls enjoyed bliss they could only dream about on earth. In either case, a proper funeral was considered essential. At one point laws were passed in various city-states, particularly in egalitarian Sparta, prohibiting lavish displays at funerals because it raised envy among poorer people. Athens also banned lavish funerals because showing off was considered undemocratic.

Many valuables have been found by archaeologists that were buried along with the deceased, including coins, which sometimes were placed in the mouth of the body to pay for the ferry trip from the land of the living to

A PLACE LIKE HEAVEN

A few lucky people, the ancient Greeks believed, might spend their afterlife in Elysium. This mythical land was the final resting place for heroes favored by the gods and was said to exist somewhere beyond the known human world. The poet Pindar said the lucky souls who reached Elysium found "the plains around their city are red with roses and shaded by incense trees heavy with fruit" (as quoted in Charles Freeman's *The Greek Achievement*). The notion of Elysium has endured in the phrase "Elysian fields," which poets and others have used as a synonym for paradise.

the underworld that lay across the mythical River Styx.

The Gods and Religion

Births, funerals, weddings, the departure of a soldier for war—all were conducted with great attention to deity-pleasing rituals. In both public and private life, religion was an integral part of everyday activities, and the gods were thought to be living beings who constantly influenced daily events. Each god had one or two areas of human endeavor or the physical world that he or she watched over. Poseidon, for example, ruled the seas, while Apollo was the god of both medicine and music. A sailor hoping for smooth waters or a doctor seeking a cure knew which god to pray to for help.

Meeting of the Gods
Poseidon, Apollo, and Artemis (left to right) converse in this relief from the east frieze of the Parthenon. The Greek gods looked much like the Greeks themselves, and had many human attributes.

The most important Greek gods and goddesses, 12 in all, were thought to be a family—the 12 Olympians—that lived atop Mt. Olympus in northern Greece, the highest spot in the land. A few other lesser gods lived there also, and elsewhere. The gods traced their roots to Gaia, the "mother Earth" that still lived beneath the Greeks. By feasting on nectar and a special food called ambrosia, the gods could live forever. (Today the word *ambrosia* can be used to describe an especially tasty food that is good enough for the gods.)

The Greek gods were a lot like the Greeks themselves. The gods ate, had families (sometimes with humans), and argued with one another. Gods could be kindly, cruel, or ridiculous. Edith Hamilton, who wrote a classic retelling of Greek myths, says in her book *Mythology* that by creating gods in their own image the Greeks' deities were comfortably familiar, even if they were sometimes fearsome.

According to the Greeks' religion, the gods played an active role in the life of humans. Festivals, rituals, sacrifices, and prayer were designed to honor the gods. In return, worshipers expected the gods to grant them favors or produce a positive result: victory in war for a city, a good harvest in a particular *deme*, or the birth of a healthy child within an individual

The Major Greek Gods and Goddesses

The 12 Olympians are not always the same dozen. Some sources do not list Hades because he moved from Mt. Olympus to the underworld). Other sources do not include Demeter, who abandoned Olympus when she found out Zeus had allowed Hades to marry her daughter, Persephone, without her permission. This list includes Demeter, for a total of 13 Olympians.

NAME	GOD OF	FAMILY ROLE	SYMBOLS
Zeus	Heaven and earth, thunder, all gods and men	Father	Lightning bolt, eagle, oak tree
Hera	Women, childbirth	Zeus' wife (and sister)	Peacock
Poseidon	Seas, earthquakes, horses	Zeus's brother	Trident, dolphin
Hades	The underworld	Zeus's brother	Pomegranates, cap of invisibility
Demeter	Agriculture, corn, marriage	Zeus's sister	Sheaves of wheat, torch
Hestia	Hearth and home	Zeus's sister	Fireplace
Aphrodite	Love, beauty	Daughter of Zeus and Dione (also said to have sprung out of sea foam)	Dove, swan, roses
Apollo	Sun, poetry, music, medicine, fine arts	Son of Zeus and Phoebus, twin brother of Artemis	Lyre, laurel tree
Ares	War	Son of Zeus and Hera	Dog, vulture
Artemis	Hunting, Moon, virgins	Daughter of Zeus and Leto; twin sister of Apollo	Deer, bow and arrows, moon
Athena	Wisdom, arts and crafts, warfare	Daughter of Zeus and Metis; emerged fully grown from her father's head	Owl, olive tree
Hephaestus	The forge, metal workers	Son of Zeus and Hera; husband of Aphrodite	Hammer
Hermes	Wealth, travelers, trade, communications, thieves, cunning	Son of Zeus and Maia	Winged sandals, caduceus (two snakes wrapped around a staff)

family. People also believed the gods could inform them about future events and heal the sick. Yet following religious traditions was not enough to protect people from misfortune. They still had to behave well toward others and follow the law. If not, they could expect something terrible to happen as punishment for their misdeeds.

The gods' active role in human affairs extended to the physical world. During a storm the Greeks would say "Zeus rains" or "Zeus thunders," because he was lord of the sky. They literally saw the immortals' footprints in their landscape, as well; they believed a mountaintop got its unusual shape because the winged horse Pegasus stamped his hoof there, and the flat outcrop of the Acropolis was where Athena and Poseidon battled to control Athens.

The Greeks did not have a single organized church that directed how people should worship. Non-religious figures–heads of households, kings, public officials–led many religious rites. The Greek religion lacked dogma– a set of strict beliefs and rules. Instead, as long as people stuck to their age-old rituals and did not reject the gods altogether (as Socrates was accused of doing), they could interpret the gods as they wished. That freedom led to less-than-flattering and even comical portrayals of the gods in myth and drama.

The lack of dogma and a highly structured religion also gave Greece's great thinkers the freedom to inquire about the nature of the universe without worrying that their ideas would offend any religious leaders. The only people thought to have direct contact with the gods, writes Robert Parker in *The Oxford History of Greece and the Hellenistic World*, were seers–people who could look into the future. But even these prophets could be ignored without risking grave harm to the community. "The seer knows," Parker says, "but the ruler decides."

Public Festivals and Rituals

Almost any time Greeks congregated as a large, mixed group, it was for a festival honoring a god or goddess. Athens's annual calendar was packed with religious festivals, taking place on almost half the days in a year. Held in honor of the city's patron deity, Athena, as well as other important deities (such as Demeter and Apollo), some festivals allowed *metics* and even slaves to participate. Other city-states had similar festivals honoring their patron god or goddess.

At the heart of a festival was the sacrifice, usually of animals but sometimes grain as well, to please the gods and stay on their good side.

Preceding the sacrifice was a procession—a huge one if it was the Panathenaea festival in Athens, held every fourth year in July when the new civic and religious calendar began. That procession began at a northwest gate in the city wall and made its way through the city along the Panathenaic Way up to the Acropolis.

Thousands of people either watching or participating in the procession accompanied a herd of cattle led to an outdoor altar at the temple to Athena on the Acropolis, where priests and priestesses conducted the opening festival rituals on behalf of the community. Only a priest or priestess could enter a temple. The public worshiped in the god's sanctuary, which was be filled with offerings from those seeking divine help. Perhaps a fine tool or piece of pottery was presented to the deity as a gift; the more valuable the offering, the more pleased, supposedly, the god or goddess would be, and the more impressed another Greek might be with one's wealth.

Sacrifices were performed outside a temple before the assembled crowd. The animals were butchered and a small portion of the meat was burnt on an altar as an offering to, in this case, Athena. Then the rest of the meat was roasted and distributed among the crowd for a communal feast. Over the course of several days Athena was then entertained by contests in choral singing, athletics, and instrumental performances.

Women in ancient Greece played their most visible public role in religion and the festivals honoring the gods. They sang in choruses at weddings and other ceremonies, sometimes after receiving special training. Sappho, the great poet (see page 92), ran a school for aristocratic girls who hoped to sing in a chorus. A festival called the Thesmophoria, which honored the goddess Demeter, was held in various cities and was exclusively for women. For three days they interacted freely, without any men controlling their actions. Of course, once the festival ended, they went back to the social reality of male dominance.

The most important public role women played was as priestesses. Like their male counterparts, priestesses were employed by the city-state to serve in the local deity's temple. The job was not full-time and priestesses did not need special skills for their work. The position of priestess did not lead to any special political or economic power, though it might boost the social standing of a woman chosen for the job. One special job for priestesses was serving as a temple's oracle. People came to the oracle seeking advice or information about the future. The priestess of the oracle went into a trance that supposedly enabled her to communicate with the temple's

FESTIVAL MENU

According to John Camp and Elizabeth Fisher in *The World of the Ancient Greeks*, a calendar from the fourth century B.C.E. revealed the sacrifices made in one Athenian village. The schedule included "for Zeus Polieus a choice sheep, a choice young pig . . . for Prokris a table of offerings . . . for Poseidon at Sounion a choice lamb, for Apollo a he-goat. . . . "

god, then provided an answer for the questioner. The most famous oracle was at the temple of Apollo at Delphi.

Arts and Athletics in Religion

Religion and the festivals it spawned led to important developments in Greek cultural life that have influenced the modern world, as well. The annual Athenian festival honoring Dionysus led to the development of Greek drama. The Greeks first celebrated the god of wine and merry-making by singing and dancing to praise him. The songs and dances then evolved into plays, with first one actor speaking to the crowd, then another, until drama was born. Theaters then appeared across the Greek world.

Music and dance continued to play key roles in the Dionysian drama. Men played all the roles, wearing costumes and masks. Playwrights entered contests to see whose play would be performed, and the winners became some of the ancient world's first celebrities. Actors and producers also won awards for their work. Aristophanes, the first great comic playwright whose work has survived, described the importance of drama to the Greeks in his play *The Frogs* (as translated by Dudley Fitts). The chorus leader says, "There is no function more noble than that of the god-touched Chorus teaching the City in song." (For more information on Greek drama and its lasting influence, see chapter 6.)

The festival honoring Zeus at Mt. Olympia, held every four years, became known as the Olympics and became the best athletics competition in Greece. Although working with one's hands was looked down upon, athletics was considered an appropriate way for men to prove their merit. It also was seen as a necessary regimen for military preparedness.

For the Olympics, male athletes and spectators arrived from all over the Greek

Perfect Form
The Discus Thrower*, sculpted in marble by Myron of Athens in the fifth century* B.C.E.*, illustrates the great value the Greeks placed on physical beauty and athletic ability. This statue is quite accurate– men competed naked in the Olympics.*

world (women were strictly forbidden to attend). Athletes arrived early to give themselves time to prove to judges they were of Greek birth. The actual competition was held in an enclosed area called the *altis*, which also featured two temples (one dedicated to Zeus and one to his wife, Hera), as well as a stadium—which comes from the Greek word *stadion*, a unit of

CONNECTIONS >>>>>>>>>>>>>>>>>>>>>>>>>>>>>>>>>>>>>

The Modern Olympics

The ancient Olympics of Greece led to the modern Olympic Games, first held in Athens in 1896. The founders of the modern games were inspired by the Greek tradition of calling a truce in any wars taking place as the Olympics were scheduled to begin. The modern Olympics were seen as a way to promote peace among nations.

Today, both winter and summer games are held, featuring hundreds of events in more than 35 sports. Athletes still compete in such Greek sports as running, boxing, and wrestling, and the Summer Olympics still has a pentathlon. In the modern event, men shoot, fence, swim, compete in horse jumping, and run. The modern games also has a decathlon with 10 track and field events (*deka* is the Greek word for "10"). The decathlon includes the discus and javelin throws from the ancient pentathlon. Women can compete in a seven-event contest called the heptathlon, which combines running, throwing, and jumping events.

Just as in ancient times, modern athletes receive only small awards for their efforts in the Olympics. But much greater riches await the top athletes, who can go on to earn money in their sport and by promoting commercial products and services.

In 2004, the Summer Olympics returned to Athens. The opening ceremony included a pageant that retold the history of ancient and modern Greece, and illustrated Greece's many lasting contributions to modern culture. Some ancient Olympian traditions were revived, as well. For example, all the medal winners received crowns of olive leaves. The marathon race began in Marathon and ended in Athens, and the shotput competition was held in the ancient sporting ground in Olympia, with spectators sitting on the grassy hillsides just as the ancient Greeks did.

But even when Greece is not hosting an Olympics, it plays a part. Greece always marches into the stadium first during the opening ceremony, no matter where the Games are held. And for both the Summer and Winter Games, a torch is lit in Olympia, using the sun's rays reflected off a mirror, and then is brought by relay runners to the site of the Games and used to light the Olympic flame. The Olympic flame traces its roots to the ancient Greek games, when a flame in honor of Zeus burned throughout the event.

measurement of about 600 feet. Spectators camped out on the surrounding plains at night, and by day crowded the grassy hillsides overlooking the stadium as runners raced back and forth, rather than around its perimeter. Stones imbedded in the ground held special starting gates—the stones are still visible today. Drawings of the games on Greek pottery show referees wielding rods to keep eager athletes from jumping the starting signals.

Athletes competed in the pentathlon, a combined contest of long jump, running, discus, and javelin throwing, and wrestling. (The name comes from the Greek words *pente*, meaning "five," and *athlon*, or "contest.") Other events included foot races of various lengths, horse and chariot races, boxing, and an event called the *pankration*. This sport was a blend of boxing and wrestling. Fighters could inflict pain in any way, except by gouging their opponent's eyes or biting.

All Olympic athletes competed as individuals, rather than as part of a city-state team. And athletes at the Olympic games not only represented physical excellence, they also represented wealth. After all, a top athlete needs plenty of time—*leisure* time—to develop his strength, speed, and agility. A typical Greek peasant farmer had no time to train for athletic competitions.

The award for Olympic champions was quite simple: Winners were crowned with a plain wreath of olive or laurel leaves. But once he returned home, the honors an athlete received could really add up, especially as the games gained in importance over the decades from their beginnings in 776 B.C.E. In fact, the Olympics inspired young men to try to become professional athletes (there were athletic contests at other festivals during the Olympics' off years). Top athletes could bring in a decent income from appearance fees and by participating in other sporting events, much as they do today.

In his book *Ancient Greece: From Prehistoric to Hellenistic Times*, Thomas Martin describes the most famous Greek sports star, Milo from Croton, a Greek city-state in southern Italy. Milo won the Olympic wrestling crown six times, beginning in 536 B.C.E., and performed stunts that included holding his breath until his bulging veins "would snap a cord tied around his head."

CHAPTER 6

Greek Art, Philosophy, and Science

THE GREEKS CREATED A BODY OF LITERATURE AND PHILOS-ophy whose impact endures into the 21st century. Norman Cantor and Peter Klein, in their introduction to *Ancient Thought: Plato and Aristotle,* echo other historians when they write, "Not only did the Greeks fashion new forms of intellectual artistic expression–tragedy, history, and philoso-phy–but they provided an entirely new set of intellectual categories through which the world could be viewed and judged." People before the Greeks thought about the nature of the world, but the Greeks left behind a written record that stimulated debate and laid a foundation for future study.

Homer and Early Literature

The foundation of ancient Greek culture was the poet Homer. Greeks re-ferred to their favorite storyteller as simply "the poet," but Homer's sig-nificance was such that several city-states claimed to be his birthplace. The stories he is credited with brilliantly retelling–the two epic poems *The Iliad* and *The Odyssey*–had been passed down orally for centuries, since Myce-naean times (for a synopsis of both, see page 19).

Homeric literature served a variety of purposes. It spoke to the Greeks of their noble past and of their special relationship with the gods who control the universe, and it gave them a sense of unity that overcame their geographic barriers and political separation. Homer's poems were of such lyrical quality that they have remained immortal, much as the gods and heroes they depict, and, along with the Bible, are considered the basis of literature in the Western world.

As Homer told the story of *The Iliad*, writes Kenneth J. Atchity in *The Classical Greek Reader*, it is not about the Trojan War as much as it is

OPPOSITE
Music of the Gods
Apollo plays the lyre, an instrument associated with him. Music was a standard part of a Greek child's education. In The Iliad, *Achilles was as skilled with his lyre as he was with his weapons. This bronze statue was found in Pompeii, a resort city in ancient Rome, and also illustrates the profound influence the Greek gods had on the development of Roman culture.*

about "repercussions of the quarrel between the mightiest Greek hero, Achilles, and . . . Agamemnon." It is a story about heroes and gods, driven by all-too-human weaknesses and misunderstandings, and it is a myth "by which the Greeks explained . . . all of life and death," writes Atchity. In the The Odyssey, the hero Odysseus introduces the concept of moral relativism (doing whatever is required at a given moment to survive), earning him Athena's admiration. "Two of a kind, we are, contrivers both," she concedes to Odysseus (quoted in *The Classical Greek Reader*).

The other significant early Greek writer was Hesiod, who worked around 700 B.C.E. He was from Boeotia, an area with rich farmland, and his book *Works and Days* dealt with agricultural life as well as his own philosophy. In it, he discussed the difference between good strife and bad strife—good strife being those challenging situations, such as competitions, that make us work harder. Bad strife, created by self-centered persons (or the gods) disrupts social harmony. Hesiod also advised that the poor should avoid violence. "The better path is to go . . . [is] towards justice; for justice beats outrage when she comes at length to the end of the race," he wrote (as posted at the Online Medieval and Classic Library). In *Theogony*, Hesiod claimed that the nine Muses (see the box on the opposite page) inspired him to retell the ancient beginnings of the gods. The religious myths he and other storytellers recorded and dramatized were inspiration for the Greeks' art and architecture.

Poetry

Sappho (d. c. 580 B.C.E.), born in Mytilene on the island of Lesbos, is considered one of the first poets to deal with personal thoughts and feelings, and was much admired by ancient Greek writers who followed her—including Plato, who called her the 10th Muse. Though a wife and mother, she often wrote of erotic feelings toward other women, and consequently members of the medieval Christian Church destroyed much of her poetry. The name of her home island was later modified into the word lesbian, meaning a woman who has sexual relations with other women, and *Sapphic* can refer either to poetry similar to Sappho's or to lesbian issues.

Pindar was an Athenian-educated Theban aristocrat whose lyric poetry was much in demand. Lyrical poetry was sung to accompaniment of the lyre, a musical instrument much like a small harp, and Pindar was the most famous and productive lyric poet of his era. What survives of his works are four books of victory odes he was commissioned to write for his fellow aristocrats, who were athletic champions. Just as it was not proper

THEN

A poem by Sappho

In gold sandals
dawn like a thief
fell upon me

(From *The Classical Greek Reader*)

for generals to boast of their military accomplishments, Pindar's musical odes did not focus on any individual's athletic achievements, but rather on the athlete's noble family or even a mythological story related to the champion's success.

The Birth of Drama

Greek drama developed as part of Athens's festival tribute to Dionysus, the son of Zeus and a mortal Theban woman. Dionysus was the god of drama and wine. Every year playwrights were chosen to present their plays, primarily tragedies at first, then comedies as well, at the festival. The tragedies were written in verse and drew heavily on Greek mythology, featuring stories of often-tragic dealings between humans and gods.

Plays were performed at an outdoor theater each spring. As many as 14,000 spectators might crowd into the Acropolis hillside that served as theater seating. The stage was a raised platform and scenery was often simple, but the actors' costumes were elaborate and there might even be special effects, such as an actor being lifted by a crane to appear to fly. The playwright was the show's director, producer, and songwriter, since the dramatic storyline was enhanced by singing parts performed by a chorus.

The first festival performances were not plays in the modern sense. The performers sang and danced to honor Dionysus, just as other ancient cultures did to honor their gods. The Greek innovation was to introduce

CONNECTIONS >>>>>>>>>>>>

The Muses

The Muses were the daughters of Zeus and Mnemosyn (which means "memory," from which we get *mnemonics*—techniques that help improve memory). Hesiod wrote of the Muses (quoted in Edith Hamilton's *Mythology*), "Their hearts are set upon song and their spirit is free from care." Even a grieving man, upon hearing their singing, "forgets his dark thoughts and remembers not his troubles."

By Roman times, each sister was said to have her own artistic subject that she watched over:

Calliope	epic poetry
Thalia	comedy
Melpomene	tragedy
Clio	history
Euterpe	lyric poetry and music
Erato	love or erotic poetry
Terpischore	dance
Polyhymnia	religious songs and music
Urania	astronomy (considered an art)

Today, artists still talk about receiving inspiration from a person or thing that serves as a muse. The names of some of the Muses are also used in English. A *calliope* is an instrument with steam-powered whistles; they were once common at circuses. Something *terpsichorean* relates to dancing. The word *muse* itself is the source for the English words *music* and *museum*.

Timeless Drama

Actress Diana Rigg stars in a 1992 London production of Euripides' play Medea. *Many Greek plays explore themes that modern audiences still find relevant.*

actors who spoke. The first Greek plays had just a single actor and a chorus, with the main emphasis still on singing and dancing. Aristotle credited Aeschylus (525–456 B.C.E.), an aristocrat from Eleusis in Attica, with creating the type of perform-ance that is familiar to theatergoers even today; Aeschylus added a sec-ond actor and downplayed the role of the chorus in his work. Aeschylus wrote 90 plays, including *Seven Against Thebes*, which inspired clas-sic films such as *The Magnificent Seven* and *The Seven Samurai*. He won many Dionysian festival com-petitions, but he was defeated in 468 B.C.E. by the 27-year-old Sophocles (c. 496–406 B.C.E.), whose plays introduced a third and later a fourth actor, expanding the importance and variety of dialogue in drama.

Euripides (480–406 B.C.E.) was another great Greek dramatist, and his plays often featured strong female roles, such as *Medea*, the story of a non-Greek woman from the kingdom of Colchis who was considered a witch. Her all-consuming love is spurned by the cool-hearted Jason, who plans to marry a Corinthian princess for the prestige it will bring him–al-though he and Medea have had two sons together. Medea eventually mur-ders Jason's bride-to-be, and then their children, yet Euripides presents her–a "barbarian"–as a sympathetic character driven to despair and rage by the cold and smug Greek Jason. A testament to the enduring appeal of Greek drama is that an English translation of *Medea* recently enjoyed a popular run in Dublin, Ireland, and then in New York on Broadway.

Comedy

The purpose of comedy was to critique politics, government, or society in a humorous way–the humor making the criticism easier to swallow. Aristophanes was the greatest of the classical Greek comic playwrights. He used humor to express his views on a number of social issues, from his de-sire for peace during Athens's darkest hour–the Peloponnesian War–to his disdain for the Sophists, traveling teachers who often challenged Athenian traditions and taught rhetoric, or the art of oral argument and persuasion.

Aristophanes did not hesitate to name names in his plays, making sport of Athens's leader Cleon, the philosopher Socrates (who supposedly took a good-natured bow during a performance of *The Clouds*), and even Dionysus, who was portrayed as a coward in *The Frogs*—which was being performed at the festival honoring Dionysus! Aristophanes wrote 40 plays, of which 11 survive. The humor in his plays ranged from slapstick to downright obscene to sophisticated and sharp. They also give us glimpses into everyday life among the ancient Greeks.

Aristophanes' work is the only surviving example of what is called old Attic comedy. Its intent was to satirize current events and discuss important ideas, using songs and the chorus as well as actors. A new style of comedy developed during the fourth century B.C.E. This new comedy eliminated the satire and the chorus, using actors to tell simple stories of people in real-life situations. Certain character types—what are called stock characters—appeared in every play. These usually included a young girl and the lover who pursued her. The best-known writer of new comedy was Menander (c. 342–292 B.C.E.). Aristotle and other ancient Greeks noted that Menander was not a particularly funny comic writer, but other playwrights praised his ability to write dialogue and show life as real people lived it. Gone were the actors playing animals and clouds, as in Aristophanes.

Menander's greatest importance came as an influence on later Roman playwrights, such as

CONNECTIONS >>>>>>>>>>>>>

Modern Theater And the Greeks

Both the form and content of ancient Greek theater survive today, and the modern English words for the two main styles of drama, *tragedy* and *comedy*, come from the Greek words *tragoidia* and *komoidia*. Aristotle studied the works of the great tragic writers and described the structure he found in his *Poetics*. He believed the plot of a play should focus on one main theme and take place over just one day. From Aristotle's writings, later playwrights came up with the idea of the "three unities" of place, time, and action: A play should be set in one location, unfold over a limited time frame (no more than one day), and focus on just one major event. Aristotle also said the purpose of dramatic tragedy is to stir fear and pity in the audience, leading to an emotional release called *catharsis*.

The three unities were held as an ideal for centuries and are still taught today, although many playwrights do not follow them. Students of theater also learn about catharsis and the role drama plays in creating an emotional tension in the audience that is released by the ending.

The plays Aristotle studied are still performed around the world. The great Greek playwrights wrote about themes that all humans understand: love, family rivalries, revenge, suffering, the horror of war.

Plautus (c. 254–184 B.C.E.) Plautus took the stock characters and situations from Athenian new comedy and added gags, puns, and physical humor. His style has influenced playwrights and comedians right up to the present day. The musical *A Funny Thing Happened on the Way to the Forum* is based on Plautus's work, using some of the same jokes that cracked up Roman audiences more than 2,000 years ago.

Recording History

Another important Greek innovation in ancient literature was recording true events–history (a word that comes from the Greek *istorie*, which means "inquiry" or "research"). The Roman statesman Cicero (106–43 B.C.E.) called Herodotus the father of history for his books about the Persian wars, which were based on actual events and personalities–unlike Homer's *The Iliad*. Herodotus's broad interests went beyond Greece, and his histories include curious facts about other cultures such as the Babylonians (they did not have doctors, Herodotus said, but rather an ill person was brought to the public square to receive advice from passersby) and the Egyptians (whose study of geometry was inspired by figuring out how much rent to charge for land by measuring it). Much of what we know today about the history of the Greek world and its neighbors comes from Herodotus.

Herodotus's competitor was Thucydides, whose subject, the Peloponnesian War, was personally familiar to him. He began recording events when the war first broke out, immediately recognizing its importance. He also added analysis and drew his own conclusions about events. He wrote in his books that he based his opinions both on what he saw and on what other eyewitnesses to events told him.

Other Greek historians who followed Herodotus and Thucydides included Xenophon who, like Thucydides, was exiled from Athens and whose history was therefore sympathetic to Sparta, and Polybius (c. 205–c. 125 B.C.E.), who wrote about the transition of the Greek world to Roman rule.

Modern historians value the Greek historians for their eyewitness accounts and insights into social and political attitudes. Yet modern readers cannot take the ancient histories as absolute truth. In some cases, the historians relied on oral sources, which might have included legends along with facts. The Greek writers also brought their own biases to what they wrote, choosing to include or exclude certain facts as they saw fit (modern historians grapple with this same issue). Still, as both literature and history, the Greek texts remain useful and entertaining.

Music

Music was indispensable to the Greeks. The god Hermes was credited with making the first lyre from a tortoiseshell when he was an infant, and the instrument was also associated with Apollo. Music was recommended by Plato as a standard part of a child's education, and in *The Iliad* Achilles was as skilled with his lyre as he was with his weapons. The old myths were sung as well as told, long before they were written down. Spartan children's first lessons in their culture were taught as songs.

The works of poets were often regarded as songs, and by the sixth century B.C.E., the performance of poetry was generally accompanied by a lyre. The simpler form of the lyre could be found in Greek homes, while a similar and more complex instrument, the *kithara*, was played by professional musicians at festival competitions.

Another type of festival performance was the *dithyramb*, a dancing chorus that evolved into drama. The word *orchestra* comes from the Greek word for "dance" (*orcheisthai*), and referred to the round stage where the chorus members performed. The *aulos*, a flute-like instrument that often had two pipes, was also popular and was often used to play dancing music, but lyre playing was especially desirable because the performer could sing and play at the same time.

Pottery as Art and History

The masks worn by the actors in Greek tragedies and comedies were quite large, with exaggerated expressions, for the benefit of audience members who were seated some distance from the stage. One reason we know this is the often-detailed decorations on Athenian pottery, the subjects of

Playing the Oldies

It is not so difficult to put on an ancient Greek drama; many of the works by Greece's top dramatists have been copied and preserved. But it is not so easy to perform a musical concert, using reproductions of ancient instruments, as it might have sounded in Classical Greece. Instruments that ancient are so fragile that they cannot be played, and there was no form of written music. But one Australian musicologist is playing musical detective to figure out what Greek music must have been like.

Michael Atherton, a professor at the University of Western Sydney, studies clues about music in ancient Greece and then tries to reproduce the sound. Some of those clues are contained in musical documents that still exist, though most have missing sections. Other clues include a few fragile and valuable instruments that have survived over the years, some descriptions from sources such as Plato and Aristotle of how different instruments sounded, and pictures of the instruments and how they were held that are painted on ancient pottery. With the help of a violinmaker, Atherton tries to build copies of the Greek instruments and then figures out how to play them.

which could be anything from mythological stories to household scenes to country farms (see page 68). Another popular art form in ancient Greece was wall painting. Though none of those works survive, we can get an idea of what the wall art looked like from copies painted onto pottery. Most of the pottery that survived the centuries intact has been found in tombs.

Corinth was the most prominent producer of Greek pottery in the seventh and eighth centuries B.C.E. The typical Greek style of black figures painted on orange or red clay vases or other containers developed in Corinth, whose potters were influenced by Near Eastern styles featuring geometric patterns and animal figures. However, the black silhouette figures on Corinthian pottery reveal little about their life or religion.

The clay in Attica contains an element, illite, that gives its pottery glaze a beautiful sheen, and by the sixth century B.C.E. Athenian pottery was the dominant product and was imitated by the Corinthians. One market-savvy Athenian craftsman, Nicosthenes (d. c. 505 B.C.E.), made a steady business of selling his work to the Etruscans in Italy by decorating his pottery with popular Etruscan themes, such as boxing and reproductions of scenes from Etruscan artwork. Some pottery was whimsical, such as the cup found in Attica and dated to about 460 B.C.E. that is shaped like a cow's hoof and painted with a scene of a farmer and his cow.

An innovation in Athenian pottery dating from about 525 B.C.E. was the reverse of the black figure drawings; figures or objects were left unpainted but were given detail by etched-in lines, while the background was painted black. These painted pots offered detailed views of life in Athens. Winners of athletic competitions often received as a prize painted vases filled with olive oil from the trees of the sacred grove of Athena in the Academy.

By the fourth century B.C.E. Athens was in decline economically and production of its famous vases died out as the pottery of southern Italy came into vogue. But fortunately, a number of painted vases survive from Athens's heyday, giving historians a vividly detailed pictorial lesson in ancient Greek life and culture.

Sculpture Transformed

The artwork of the ancient Greeks began on a small scale with intricately carved jewelry that has been found dating to the 10th and ninth centuries B.C.E. While Greek potters were producing more and more naturalistic images on their wares, Greek sculptors were gaining confidence and skill working with stone. The first Greek sculptor of note was the legendary Daedalus (see the box on page 101), who perhaps lived in the late Bronze

Age. A style of sculpture featuring small, abstract figures with triangular faces is called Daedalic in his honor, though the unknown artists who made them were influenced by the art of the Near East. Sixth-century B.C.E. Greek sculpture looked Egyptian: strait-backed, stylized nude male figures called *kouros* faced forward with arms down at their sides and the left foot slightly in front of the right. A female version was a draped figure, and was usually placed in cemeteries. Eventually, relief sculpture (three-dimensional images that emerge from a flat or curved surface) began to be added to the bases of the *kouroi* statues.

By the fifth century B.C.E., Greek artists and writers were aware that the Greeks were building a new political and military force in the world, and they wanted to both honor their culture and distance themselves from the foreign models they had once copied. In sculpture, this led to greater realism and the depiction of action, as in the Discobolus ("discus thrower") sculpted by Myron of Eleutherae (c. 490–430 B.C.E.). Like all of his work, it was cast in bronze, but the only versions of it remaining are Roman copies in marble (see page 112). Sculptor Polyclitus (464–420 B.C.E.) spent his long career in Argos, where he ran a school. His sculpture was representative of the Greek admiration for symmetry, or balanced proportions, in art or architecture. The Greeks believed symmetry reflected perfection and that humans should imitate it in their art. Polyclitus's statue Doryphorus, or "spear-bearer," shows a muscular man with a taut arm and relaxed leg on one side of the body, while the figure's other arm and leg are just the opposite.

The style of Polyclitus fit into an ideal of Greek art that dated back to the *kouros*, of trying to represent the perfect body in art. Polyclitus began a trend among sculptors, who copied his proportions and began featuring more humans, rather than deities, in their work. Attention to every detail of the subject matter, such as the folds on a cloak, showed the great technical skill developed during this period, and influenced artists for centuries to come.

Polyclitus and his competitor Phidias (c. 500–c. 432 B.C.E.) were the masters during the Classical period of Greek art. The Roman historian Pliny the Elder (23–79 C.E.) wrote that from Polyclitus's statue the Canon, other sculptors "derive the basic forms of their art, as if from some kind of law" (quoted in *The Art of Ancient Greece* by J. J. Pollitt).

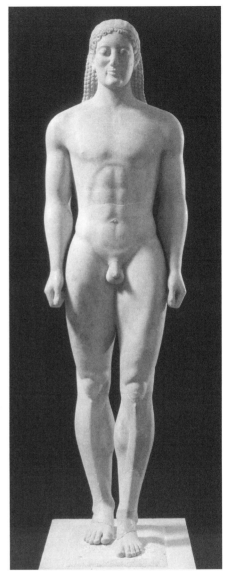

Formal Portrait
This kouros *from Attica (c. 525 B.C.E.) illustrates the stiff, formal style the early Greeks favored. Contrast it with the very natural sculpture on page 87—a style that revolutionized art.*

DORIC   IONIC   CORINTHIAN

Columns in Order

The Greek styles of architecture are called orders, and are easy to tell apart by their different column styles. All three styles are still widely used today.

Architecture

The two main styles of architecture in ancient Greece were Doric, which dominated temples and other public buildings on the Greek mainland, and Ionic, which was prevalent in Ionia and on the islands in the Aegean. Today in architecture, the two styles are called *orders*. The orders are perhaps most easily identified by the types of columns used. Doric columns are wider, sturdier, and more simply styled than the slimmer, more decorative Ionic columns.

A third order, Corinthian, was first used primarily inside temples. It dates from the fifth century B.C.E. and its columns are similar to the ones in the Ionic order, although the tops of the Corinthian columns are more ornate. Roman architects later popularized the use of the Corinthian order on the outside of buildings, and they are still used today in buildings designed in the Classical style.

The most readily available building materials in ancient Greece were stone and wood. In Corinth, the cultural center of early Archaic Greece, a temple for Poseidon was made entirely of stone. Its walls were then covered with stucco and painted with geometric designs and figures. As Greece grew more prosperous, marble was preferred, despite the higher cost of quarrying and transporting it. Athens was fortunate to discover a large source of marble just to the north at Mount Pentelikon. The city also had increasing wealth, thanks to money coming in from the Delian League after the Persian Wars and from the Laurium silver mines, so it could afford this expensive material.

Given the ready supply of marble and Athenian wealth, Pericles was able embark on a building program that proclaimed his city the leader among Greeks. The premier new building was the Parthenon, dedicated to Athena (although construction of a new temple for the goddess had actually begun during the years of the Persian War, before the destruction of the Acropolis). Athena's new temple was Doric in style and richly decorated with a 524-foot frieze, or sculpted band, around the top of the building. The frieze featured a single scene: the great procession through Athens that began the Panathenaic festival. The procession is shown moving from two starting points, finally meeting in the center of the eastern side, which was over the temple's entrance. The temple also has 92 intricately carved panels called *metopes*, and two carved column pediments, which are triangular pieces between the roof and the columns on the building's front and back. The *metopes* were painted in bright colors and depict mythological battles that proclaim the triumph of the Greek culture over barbarians, as in the Greeks' defeat of the Persian Empire.

Although today surviving Greek sculptures or later copies are in natural white marble, in their ancient state the statues and architectural friezes were painted in vivid colors. So the Parthenon was not just an architectural marvel; it also featured an explosion of color, which must have been especially dramatic against the sunny, blue-sky backdrop of southern Greece.

Other new buildings on the Acropolis were the Erechtheum, an irregularly shaped building whose interior honored several deities, and the smaller Athena Nike (victory) temple, on whose walls was a large painting depicting the victory at Marathon.

Altogether, construction on the Acropolis lasted nearly half a century, from about 450 to 405 B.C.E. We know about the building processes—what kind of craftsmen were used, how much they were paid—because detailed records engraved in marble have survived. More importantly, the ruins of the whole project survive. "Mighty indeed are the marks and monuments of our empire which we have left," said Pericles of the Acropolis (as quoted in *The Cambridge Illustrated History of Ancient Greece*). "Future ages will wonder at us as the present age wonders now."

CONNECTIONS >>>>>>>>>>>>

Artist, Architect, Engineer

Daedalus's name means "cunning fabricator." He was an architect and engineer as well as an artist, and the ancient Greeks credited him with several inventions, including the axe and sails for ships. Today Daedalus is known as the main character in several important Greek myths.

On the island of Crete, he is said to have built the first labyrinth, a maze of passageways and dead-ends, that contained the Minotaur, a monstrous bull. Daedalus also built a set of wings for himself and his son Icarus, so they could escape Crete after its king imprisoned them. The wings were made of bird feathers and wax, and Daedalus instructed his son not too fly to close to sun because the wax would melt. Icarus ignored his father's advice and plunged to his death.

Designed by two builders, Ictinus (fifth century B.C.E.) and Callicrates (fifth century B.C.E.), the Parthenon employed some visual tricks that required great technical skills. For example, columns, when placed perfectly vertical, actually appear to be leaning slightly outward, so the Parthenon's columns were angled slightly inward to appear to be at a 90-degree angle to the ground. Also, to the human eye columns appear to be slightly tapered in the middle, so the actual columns had a slight bulge added to them in the center to compensate. Each column was made from sections, or drums, of marble stacked one atop the other, so each drum had to be cut precisely at slightly different angles, since the entire column had to lean inward. And the images sculpted into the frieze, placed high atop the building, would have been difficult for temple visitors to see, so the top part of the frieze was carved about two inches deeper than the bottom part.

The buildings erected on the Acropolis and across Greece had a lasting impact on Western architecture. The Romans copied the various orders and the Greek fondness for monumental public buildings that inspired awe for the gods and enshrined the Greek values of order and balance. From the Renaissance through modern times, architects have turned back to these Greco-Roman ideals. The ancient styles are often used in buildings that are thought to be "temples" to such things as government, academics, and commerce. For example, the U.S. Supreme Court Building in Washington, D.C., with its pediments and Corinthian columns, reveals the importance its occupants play in the American legal system. In New York, the U.S. Stock Exchange, another temple-like structure, is famous for the sculpture on its pediment showing Integrity as a woman protecting the inventions of humanity. Across Europe and North America today, many legislative buildings and parliaments echo the ancient Greco-Roman architectural styles, connecting the present systems of government to the greatness of Athenian democracy.

Pondering the Universe

Classical Athens was home to philosophy schools that drew students from all over Greece and, later, the Roman Empire. The great teachers of Athens remain some of the best-known thinkers today: Socrates, Plato, and Aristotle. At their schools, and at others, students learned mathematics, botany, biology, and astronomy, as well as philosophy–the study of human values and knowledge.

But Athens was not where the study, and indeed the very idea of philosophy began. The first Greek philosophers came from Miletus, a city in Ionia. In the sixth century B.C.E. these thinkers started formally studying questions that humanity had been pondering for centuries: What is the universe all about and what is the role of humans in it. Once again, the Greeks were inspired by knowledge they obtained from others–in this case, the Babylonians' advanced knowledge of astronomy. The Babylonians had detailed records of the movement of stars and planets and could accurately predict their future movements, suggesting the universe had some kind of order. The Greek thinkers, however, were not content to just record what they saw and make predictions; they wanted to understand why the universe operated as it did. They then also began to ask "why" and "how" for events in the physical world and in the thought processes of humans.

The Greeks' studies were very original, because people had always assumed the answers were found in religion–it thunders because Zeus is angry, or people should behave a certain way because it pleases the gods. But the first philosophers were skeptical of divine interpretations of the natural world and believed they could discover the order of the universe through observation and thought, leading to science and philosophy. Early on, these two fields were closely linked. Philosopher-scientists asked, what is our world and the life in it made of? What is reality and what is perception? The answers to these questions combined scientific theory and observation with creative reasoning.

The First Philosophers

CONNECTIONS >>>>>>>>>>>

Nashville's Parthenon

Today Athens's Parthenon is an ancient ruin. But to get an idea of what the Parthenon might have looked like in its glory days in Athens, head to Nashville, Tennessee. The city of Nashville built a full-scale replica of the Parthenon in 1897 for the 100th anniversary celebration of Tennessee statehood. Surrounded by a large city park, it originally it was made of plaster, wood, and brick, but was rebuilt in 1920 of concrete.

For more information on the Nashville Parthenon, visit the city of Nashville web site at www.nashville.gov/parthenon/ or write to The Nashville Parthenon, The Parthenon Centennial Park, Nashville, Tennessee, 37201.

Thales of Miletus (c. 640–546 B.C.E.) was the first known philosopher. He came up with the theory that water is the essence of life and reality–ignoring for the first time the idea that the gods might have something to do with reality, too. Thus he is credited with originating the field of physical science. Anaximander (c. 610–546 B.C.E.) followed Thales, possibly as his student, but disagreed with Thales' water theory, suggesting that the substance of the universe and the life in it is unidentifiable. He also said our world is but one of many. Anaximander was followed by his student, Anaximenes (c. 590–525 B.C.E.), who defined his teacher's unidentifiable substance as air–an idea he based on observing the evaporation of water, or water "changing into air." Even the human soul consists of air, Anaximenes said. These three men from Miletus, though their theories might sound overly simple today, were quite revolutionary in suggesting that human beings can use their own reasoning and observations to come up with the definition of life itself.

Another great thinker from Ionia was Pythagoras, though his greatest fame came from work he did after he left his homeland. He believed the universe could be explained through mathematics and taught that souls were immortal and entered new bodies after people died, and that a person's actions in life influenced what kind of body his or her soul would later next. He also developed what seems today like a cult. A group of

The Pythagorean Theorum

Pythagoras and his followers also did important work in mathematics, and Pythagoras is best known today for the theorem that bears his name. Students around the world learn that the sum of the squares of the length of each side of a right triangle equals the square of the length of the hypotenuse: $a^2 + b^2 = c^2$. With this formula, a person can determine the length of any side of a right triangle if he or she knows the length of the other two sides.

students, both men and women, lived with him apart from Greek society. The Pythagoreans were vegetarians and avoided the usual Greek religious rites.

The Ionians were followed in the fifth century B.C.E. by other philosopher-scientists who continued to challenge their predecessors' ideas about the universe and the nature of reality. Parmenides (b. 510 B.C.E.) was significant for suggesting that the input from human senses should be put aside in favor of reasoning to answer questions about the universe, which he considered to be an unchanging, fixed entity, despite what our senses might tell us. His challenge, then, to future philosophers was to use intellectual methods to support their notions of reality, as well as their observations. Another Ionian, Pericles' friend Anaxagorus (c. 500–428 B.C.E.), said change is inevitable because of minute particles that are always in constant flux. These particles, or seeds, made up everything that existed, forming different combinations to create such diverse things as a person and a dog. His arguments were expanded on by other philosophers, who said the small particles could not be divided into smaller particles, and were in constant motion. In Greek, these particles were called *a-toma*, or "uncuttable," which led to the English words *atom* and *atomic*. Modern science has shown that the Greek atomists were right about the idea of indivisible particles that comprise all matter in the universe.

A Battle Over Ethics

Socrates (470–399 B.C.E.), an Athenian, is credited with steering philosophy toward the study of morality and ethics. In a city that valued beauty and wealth, Socrates was unusual. He came from humble birth and chose to remain poor, and with his bulging eyes and turned-up nose he was homely, something he readily admitted. Although he had supported his wife and children as a stonemason and served Athens as a hoplite, he spent his later years wandering through the city, making it his work to engage citizens in friendly but pointed discussions about justice, courage, and other moral issues. He did not ask for payment from those he informally taught.

His discussions involved leading his conversation partner through a variety of questions, often arriving at unexpected conclusions. By asking questions, Socrates forced his listeners to draw their own conclusions, though with his wisdom guiding the direction of the argument. Though skilled at argument, Socrates would not claim to know the answers to the questions he asked. This style of teaching is today called the *Socratic method* and is still used, primarily in law schools but also in other fields of study. Perhaps his most famous line, as reported by Plato in his *Apology* (quoted in *The Last Days of Socrates*), is, "The unexamined life is not worth living."

Socrates was concerned with questions of right and wrong, which set him apart from a group called the Sophists-traveling teachers-for-hire who were specialists in the art of rhetoric. Public speaking was an important skill for Greek aristocrats: One may have wanted to sway Assembly voters on a particular issue, be persuasive in court, or impress other influential men at a symposium. The Sophists vowed to take students beyond rhetoric and teach them how to use logic to turn any argument in their favor. The Sophists were especially popular with would-be politicians, but they came under criticism for their tendency to disregard right and wrong in favor of winning arguments.

Socrates and his students, particularly Plato, opposed the Sophists and their methods of argument. Like his teacher, Plato sought the virtuous and ideal. His earlier writings were in the form of dialogues that often featured Socrates as one of the speakers and explained much of what Socrates taught. Plato also developed his own notion of forms. He believed that for every real, physical thing that existed, there was a corresponding form that was the ideal of that thing, and the ideal form existed even if the real thing did not. For example, the form of a chair was distinct from the real chairs that people sat on, though those chairs had qualities of the form. Forms could also apply to human traits, such as

Great Thinker
Socrates explored important issues with his students by asking them pointed questions. This style of teaching is still used today, and is known as the Socratic method.

Death of a Philosopher

Jovial and a larger-than-life character with many influential friends, Socrates stirred suspicion in many Athenians. They accused him of destroying the morals of the city's youth with his teachings, which his critics claimed encouraged people to reject the traditional Greek gods and discover new ways of explaining human existence. Though the ancient Greeks had no real religious rules to disobey in the first place, in the aftermath of the Peloponnesian War many Athenians were insecure about their relationship with the gods.

Socrates was a target because of his refusal to follow convention. He also had a following of young men who were opposed to democracy, and some of them later became major figures among the 30 Tyrants (see page 41). There was a general political amnesty in 403 B.C.E., so no one could directly accuse Socrates of supporting the 30 (in fact, he had openly disobeyed them), but his trial was an attempt to get back at Socrates for what was perceived to be his bad influence on Athenian youth.

In 399 B.C.E., by a narrow majority, a jury of about 500 men convicted Socrates of introducing new gods and corrupting the youth of Athens. He chose execution rather than admit wrongdoing and go into exile, and drank the poison hemlock, which was commonly used for suicide at the time.

virtue. A person could have attributes of the form of virtue, though they could never be completely virtuous. If this sounds a little strange to you, it did to the ancient Athenians as well.

Plato also wrote about politics and society, and his book *Republic and Laws* contained many suggestions on how to achieve the ideal political state, covering not just government but also education and religion. Plato disliked traditional Athenian democracy, because he believed most people lacked the intelligence and moral character to rule wisely. He thought "philosopher kings" should rule, educating others in the right way to behave for the good of all society. Plato wrote in his *Republic*, "The law is not concerned with the special happiness of any class in the state, but in trying to produce this condition in the city as a whole, harmonizing and adapting the citizens to one another by persuasion and compulsion. . . ." (quoted in Norman Cantor and Peter L. Klein's *Ancient Thought: Plato and Aristotle*).

Aristotle

Just as Plato was considered Socrates' most brilliant student, Aristotle was Plato's. Aristotle arrived at Athens at age 17 from his home in northern

Greece to study with Plato. Aristotle's interests were vast; he not only continued the philosophical discussion of virtue and ethics that he learned from Plato, but also conducted groundbreaking research in the natural sciences. Aristotle is also considered the first philosopher of science, as he tried to separate philosophy, which is the study of ideas, from science, the study of the natural world. He was the first person to try to spell out what science is and how it should be conducted.

As Paul K. Feyerbend writes in *The Oxford Companion to Philosophy*, Aristotle "tried to reconcile observations, common sense and abstract thought" and "described how facts turn into concepts, and further, into principles." Aristotle wrote in *The Physics*, (included in Cantor and Klein's *Ancient Though: Plato and Aristotle*) "[I]n the study of nature . . . our first object must be to establish principles." Only by knowing the principles and causes of the natural world could humans truly understand it.

Mathematics

Many thinkers whose names are not remembered today created theorems to explain the rules of geometry, and these theorems rested on proofs that followed logical arguments. Some time around 300 B.C.E., the mathematician Euclid (c. 325–c. 265 B.C.E.) took the existing proofs and theorems and collected them into one set that became the foundation of geometry for the next two millennia. His most famous work is *The Elements*. Plane and solid geometry, taken together, are still called Euclidean geometry. Another kind of geometry that deals with curved surfaces is called non-Euclidean geometry.

Another great Greek scientist and mathematician of the Hellenistic period was Archimedes (c. 287–212 B.C.E.). Levers had long been used to lift heavy objects. Archimedes took it upon himself to create a mathematical explanation for how long a lever should be to make it easier to lift a given weight. He also gave the first theoretical explanation of pi, the number that begins with 3.14 and continues forever. In math, it is still indicated by the Greek letter π. Pi is part of the formula used to find the circumference and area of a circle.

Archimedes was an active inventor, unlike most Greek scientists, who preferred to deal with abstract ideas. They considered it beneath their position as great thinkers to work as engineers or inventors. Archimedes is thought to be the inventor of a large screw that bears his name. Turning the screw moved a fluid from a low spot to a higher one. The Archimedes screw is still sometimes used today in remote areas to draw water out of ponds and wells.

WISE OR DECEPTIVE?
The Greek form of the word *sophist* meant "wise man" and suggested a teacher of wisdom, but it could also imply a cleverness that was meant to deceive. Today, *sophist* and the related English word *sophistry* still have unfavorable connotations. A modern sophist is not a teacher of any kind, but a public figure who skillfully uses words to confuse an audience, and sophistry is the faulty reasoning that person uses.

Another related word, *sophisticate*, originally had a similar meaning—to try to deceive or make an issue complex, rather than simple. Today, the adjective *sophisticated* means something that is complex, or a person who has wide experiences in the finer things of life, such as the arts or fine cuisine.

Greek Medicine

Traditionally, the Greeks were like many ancient people. They discovered herbal cures and blended them with superstitions about sickness coming from evil spirits or the gods. The Greek doctor Hippocrates (c. 460–c. 337 B.C.E.) was the first person to try to make medicine a true science. (Historians say that the writings attributed to him may have come from more than one source; Charles Freeman in his book *The Greek Achievement* refers to the "Hippocratic doctors," rather than one person of that name.)

By Hippocrates' time, doctors were already rejecting the idea that magic or other supernatural forces could cause or cure illness. Hippocrates then began applying reason and observation to the human body and illness, just as philosophers did with the universe as a whole. Some of his conclusions were wrong, such as the notion that four fluids, called humors, controlled human health, and that an imbalance of the humors caused disease. But Hippocrates and his followers did get some things right. They believed that good diet and exercise were the keys to health, and that in many cases the body could heal itself without the need for drugs.

One of Hippocrates' his lasting contributions to medicine is known today as the Hippocratic Oath. Doctors after Hippocrates swore to Apollo and the other gods that they would not harm their patients. Today, most graduating medical school students swear to some form of the oath, usually a modern version. Hippocrates' reference to the gods has been removed, but the basic premises of the oath remain the same. Doctors swear to treat the sick to the best of their ability, preserve patient privacy, teach the secrets of medicine to the next generation, and act with compassion.

The Greek scientist Herophilus (c. 335–280 B.C.E.) added to the understanding of the human body by dissecting corpses. He showed for the first time that the

CONNECTIONS >>>>>>>>>>>>

A Scientist's Words

Along with his scientific contributions, Archimedes is known today for popularizing two phrases. He supposedly ran out of his house—naked, coming out of the bath—after making a scientific discovery, shouting the word *eureka* ("I have found it!"). Today, eureka can be used when making any important discovery, and it is the motto of the state of California, referring to the discovery of gold there in 1848. Archimedes also said, regarding his study of levers, "Give me where to stand, and I will move the earth" (quoted in *Bartlett's Familiar Quotations*). Since that time, a wide range of writers and speakers—from Thomas Jefferson to former vice president Al Gore—have alluded to Archimedes' claim, and his idea that the right tools and knowledge can accomplish the seemingly impossible.

CONNECTIONS >>>>>>>>>>>>>>>>>>>>>>>>>>>>>>

The Academic Disciplines

Today's schools break down scientific study into separate areas. Many of these classifications can be traced directly to Aristotle. He was the first person to talk about biology, the study of life, and then break it down further into zoology, the study of animals. He also created the idea of a formal study of the operations of the *polis*, leading to the discipline we call politics or political science. (The word *politics* comes from the Greek *politika*, which means "things of the *polis*"—that is, doing government.)

Aristotle separated mathematics from the study of the physical world—two disciplines that had previously been joined. (The word *mathematics* comes from the Greek word *mathematikos*, meaning "to learn.") He then further divided math into arithmetic, plane geometry (the study of two-dimensional shapes) and solid geometry (the study of three-dimensional shapes). Even within philosophy, Aristotle narrowed down specific categories. He coined the term *metaphysics*, which is the branch of philosophy concerned with what is truly real and the nature of being. Metaphysics is still studied today, and *metaphysical* sometimes has a broader meaning, referring to things that are supernatural or beyond a person's usual perception of reality.

Aristotle was also the formal founder of a branch of philosophy called *logic*. In a broad sense, logic is the rational thought humans use to solve problems. Aristotle developed rules of logic and logical argument. He created the syllogism, which sets up an order of thought with three statements. Once the first idea is accepted as true, particular ideas related to it can be shown to be true or false. The classic example is, "All men are mortal. Greeks are men; therefore, all Greeks are mortal." The first two statements are called the premises, while the last is the conclusion. Aristotle's thinking is also called deductive reasoning, or drawing a particular conclusion from general true statements. Its opposite is inductive reasoning, which moves from a particular true statement to a general conclusion. Both kinds of reasoning are still taught today.

veins and arteries carried blood through the body, and he realized that a pulse was connected to a person's heart beat and that the speed could change depending on a person's health. Herophilus was also the first person to detect nerves and discover that they connected to the brain. He has been called the founder of anatomy, the study the structure of the human body.

Epilogue

ALTHOUGH THE ROMAN EMPIRE DEFEATED THE GREEK city-states in the second century B.C.E., Greek culture had already conquered the Roman Empire. The two civilizations had been acquainted since the eighth century B.C.E., when the first Greek colony was founded on Italy's west coast. When Greek cities in Greece itself, Asia Minor, and the Middle East came under Roman dominance, they kept their Greek language and culture. Roman political control was placed on top of a Hellenized society.

Culture Conquers the Conquerors

The Romans had mixed feelings about their conquered neighbors. On the one hand, they eagerly took advantage of Greek contributions in arts and science and borrowed heavily from Greek mythology. Athens and the Hellenized Egyptian city of Alexandria remained centers of higher education, and most educated people spoke Greek. The first Roman emperor, Augustus (63 B.C.E.–14 C.E.), wrote his memoirs in Greek, and the Romans absorbed many Greek words into Latin. Yet educated Greek speakers such as Augustus tried not to publicly display too much admiration for Greece. The Romans felt pride in their own accomplishments, and some Romans considered the Greeks to be immoral and inferior.

Romans might have decried how Hellenized they became, but their embrace of Greek culture helped spread it to new parts of the world. At its peak, the Roman Empire stretched from Great Britain to the Middle East, from North Africa to Germany. The Romans did not conquer as wide a swath as Alexander had, but their control endured longer. Through that dominance, a culture known today as Greco-Roman combined the best that both Rome and Classical Greece had to offer.

OPPOSITE

Olympics Come Home
A performer is dressed as a classical Greek statue during the opening ceremony of the 2004 Olympic Games in Athens. Some 10,000 athletes representing 202 countries took part in the two-week sporting competition that originated in ancient Greece.

In Roman society, Greeks held a number of important jobs, though they often performed their duties as slaves. The Greeks dominated medicine, thanks to the early influence of Hippocrates and his followers (see chapter 6). After Hippocrates, the most important physician of the classical world was Galen (129–c. 200 C.E.). Born in the Greek city of Pergamum, he came to Rome around 164 C.E. Galen proved, among other things, that urine flows from the kidneys, and he wrote the first major book on anatomy. For centuries, doctors in Europe and the Middle East considered him their most influential source.

Ptolemy (c. 90–c. 168 C.E.) was a famous Greek mathematician and astronomer. He wrote a book that argued that the sun and planets revolve around Earth. He was wrong, but his idea was accepted for almost 1,500 years, and the word *Ptolemaic* refers to his system for explaining the workings of the universe.

Early Christianity and the Greeks

Greek culture particularly thrived in the eastern parts of the Roman Empire, where the Greeks had carried out extensive trade and which Alexander had conquered. By the first century C.E., Rome had political control over the Jewish land of Judaea, located in what is now Israel and Jordan.

In this Jewish land influenced by Romans and Greeks, a new monotheistic (belief in one god) religion emerged: Christianity. Jesus Christ spoke the Middle Eastern language of Aramaic, but the followers who spread his teachings wrote and spoke primarily in Greek, the common language of the eastern Roman Empire. Later debates about Christianity's doctrines took place in Greek, and, according to Thomas Cahill in *Sailing the Wine-Dark Sea*, reflected the kind of issues ancient Greek philosophers addressed, such as the nature of matter and spirit. Cahill writes, "The two great rivers of our cultural patrimony—the Greco-Roman and Judeo-Christian—flow into each other to become the mighty torrent of Western civilization."

By 395 C.E. the Roman Empire had split in half, reunited, and then split again. The eastern portion, including Greece, was ruled from Constantinople (now Istanbul). Even before this point, the Greek-speaking east was becoming the economic and political center of the empire, and it was the seat of four of the five bishops of the Christian Church, who were based in Constantinople, Alexandria, Jerusalem, and Antioch, Syria. Rome and the western half of the empire fell to invaders in 476 C.E. The greatness that had been Rome lived on in the more Hellenized east, which became known as the Byzantine Empire.

SAVING SCULPTURE

Modern art lovers are fortunate that Rome was so enamored of its Greek lands and their culture, since the Romans helped preserved the Greek artistic tradition. Much of the Greeks' free standing sculpture was cast in bronze, most of which did not last. Roman artists made copies of these works in marble, and many of them still exist today.

The Byzantine emperors were aware that they carried on two great cultural traditions. Rome had been famous for its highly developed system of laws and courts, as well as efficient government and skilled engineering. The Byzantines also knew their roots went back even further, to the greatness of Classical Greece and its art, science, and philosophy. Greek scholars in the Byzantine Empire kept that intellectual tradition alive when the West entered into its own Dark Age, when wars continued to erupt and only a handful of Christian monks knew the basics of reading and writing.

CONNECTIONS >>>>>>>>>>>>

Importance of Logos

Dialogues were at the heart of Plato's writing, and at the heart of the word *dialogue* is the Greek word *logos*. In a general sense, *logos* means "word" or "speech." The prefix *dia* means "through," "apart," or "across," so a dialogue features words sent across from one person to another. To the ancient Greeks, *logos* also had a deeper meaning: the reason or order that controls the universe. Early Christian writers used *logos* to mean the literal word of Jesus Christ, as well as the order and wisdom he represented for the universe. *Logos* is still used that way today.

The Rise of Islam

During those centuries and beyond, ancient Greek culture was absorbed by another people: the Arabs. In the seventh century, Muhammad (c. 570–632), a merchant from Arabia (now Saudi Arabia) founded a new religion called Islam. Muhammad and his followers set out on wars of religious conquest. Soon the Islamic Arabs dominated the Middle East, North Africa, and part of Spain. Their lands included parts of what had been the old Greek, Persian, and Roman Empires.

Through their expansion, the Arabs and the people they ruled came into contact with the Byzantine Empire. Islamic scholars began to translate works by Aristotle, Plato, and other Greeks into Arabic. The scholars also read Greek texts on medicine, science, and math, and combined what they learned with ideas from Iran and India.

From the 700s through the 1200s, the Arabs battled Western kingdoms that arose from the remains of Rome's empire The Arabs also clashed with the Byzantine Empire. Yet the despite their conflicts with the descendants of Greece and Rome, the Arabs played a key role in the development of modern Western culture. Latin scholars in Western Europe knew that the Arabs had access to works that had been lost in the West, due to wars and Christian leaders who destroyed "pagan" teachings. Both

Arabic translations of ancient Greek works and original Arabic studies influenced by the Greeks were eventually translated into Latin. Western scholars finally had a chance to discover the wisdom of ancient Greece.

The Ottomans and Independence

The Arabs did not conquer the Byzantine Empire, but another Islamic people, the Ottoman Turks, did. The Turks came out of Central Asia and settled in Asia Minor, and under their ruler Osman I (1259–1324) they slowly began taking over Byzantine territory. By the mid-15th century, the Turks' rule extended into the Balkans, and in 1453 they captured Constantinople, ending the Byzantine Empire. The Turks renamed the city Istanbul and made it the capital of their Ottoman Empire. After their victory, they rampaged through the city, destroying many Greek documents, including the only surviving copies of ancient Greek works, such as plays by Euripides.

Once again, the Greeks were under foreign control, and they would remain part of this new Islamic Ottoman Empire for almost 400 years. The Turks, however, let the Greeks practice Christianity, and a class of educated Greeks served in the Ottoman government. Greeks also played an important role as traders, and Greek priests and monks had ties with Orthodox Christian leaders across Eastern Europe.

Educated Greeks in the Turkish empire kept alive the memory of ancient Greece, and they also fueled calls for independence. Many Europeans, who had rediscovered Classical Greek literature and philosophy, saw how important Greece had been in shaping Western culture. Some writers and intellectuals believed the people who had given the world so much should once again have their own nation.

In 1821, a group of Greeks rebelled against the Ottoman Empire. That revolution failed, but by 1830, with help from other European nations, Greece became an independent nation—this time a unified one. Two years later, the Greeks crowned a Bavarian prince, Otto, as their first king, in the hopes that his connections would help bind the new country to the more established nations in Europe.

Greece Today

As an independent nation, Greece has gone through difficult times. Internal struggles led to several changes in kingship, and the country was caught up in various Balkan wars and World War I. During World War II, Nazi Germany occupied Greece. After the Germans were driven out in 1944, a civil

SEEKING TRUTH

An early Islamic philosopher, al-Kindi (c. 801–866) expressed the Arabs' enthusiasm for knowledge coming from the Greeks. He wrote (as cited by Albert Hourani in *A History of the Arab Peoples*), "We should not be ashamed to acknowledge truth from whatever source it comes to us, even if it is brought to us by former generations and foreign peoples." Then, in a sentiment that echoes the values of Socrates and Aristotle, he added, "For him who seeks the truth there is nothing of higher value than truth itself."

war followed. On one side were those who supported communism, a political system marked by one-party rule and government ownership of all property and businesses. Their opponents supported Western-style democracy (and the Greek monarchy) and private ownership of property. The struggle was violent and bitter.

The democratic forces eventually won, and in 1949 the Greeks established a government with both a king and elected lawmakers. During the 1960s this government was replaced by a military dictatorship, which lasted until 1974, when important military leaders backed a return to civilian rule. The next year the Greeks wrote a new constitution that established a republic, ending the role of the monarchy.

Today Greece is a member of the European Union and the North Atlantic Treaty Organization (NATO). The economy still features elements of its ancient past: The Greeks have the world's largest fleet of merchant ships. And Greek farmers still raise grain and olives, just as they have for thousands of years. Yet the Greeks are also building a modern nation, putting more emphasis on telecommunications and industry. Perhaps most important to the economy is tourism, as people from around the world come to explore one of the historic hearts of Western civilization.

The Legacy of Ancient Greece

This book has detailed many of the concrete legacies of the Greeks: the words and concepts they used that are still common today; lasting works of art and mythological tales that inspire new generations; systems of thought that are still taught in schools. Equally important is the Greek spirit, one that questioned why the world and its the people are the way they are, and that championed original thought in seeking answers, rather than merely accepting what others said.

That spirit of open inquiry lives on in many forms, thanks to the Greek writings that have endured for more than 2,500 years. The great writings of Aristotle and others were housed at the Library in Alexandria, Egypt, whose entire collection "laid the foundations of Western learning . . . from literature to astronomy, from medicine to historiography," according to Paul Cartledge in *The Cambridge Illustrated History of Ancient Greece*. Part of that vast body of knowledge was lost to Western Europe during the Dark Ages, but the best of Athens and Rome slowly reemerged and spread to a wider audience than ever before. That reemergence rested on two developments, one technical and one intellectual. In the 15th century, German goldsmith Johannes Gutenberg invented a printing press that

GREEK MOONS

In 1610, using a telescope of his own design, Galileo discovered four moons circling the planet Jupiter. Astronomers have since found dozens more orbiting that large planet and have given them names taken from Greek mythology. The first moons Galileo saw were named for three women who had relationships with Zeus (Jupiter is his Roman name): Io, Callisto, and Europa. The fourth, Ganymede, was named for a young Trojan man whom Zeus brought to Olympus to serve the gods.

The word *planet* itself has Greek roots, coming from the word *planes* meaning "wanderer" and reflecting what the ancient Greeks realized—that the planets did not follow an orderly, circular path through the heavens. Modern scientists showed the Greeks were right: The planets orbit in a changing elliptical path, not a perfect circle.

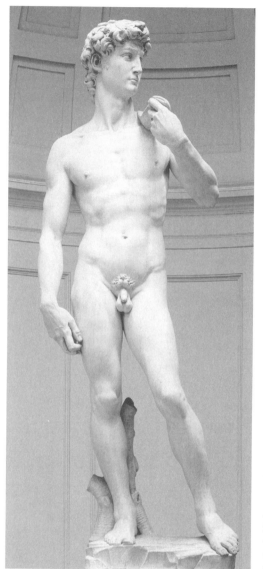

Perfect Form
Michelangelo's (1475–1564) brilliant sculpture of David marked a high point in Renaissance art. The word Renaissance *means "rebirth," and refers to the rebirth of Classical Greek ideals.*

used movable type, bringing publishing to Europe. For the first time, people could buy books, and printers created the first copies of ancient texts for European audiences. That development spurred the rise of literacy, as people sought to read in their own language. Ancient Greek writings translated and published in books reached a wider audience than any of the classic authors could have dreamed possible.

The intellectual trend that fueled an interest in the classics was the Renaissance. During the 14th century, Italy was dominated by powerful city-states—just as in ancient Greece. The Italian city-states had thriving economies, and wealthy families gave money to artists and scholars. These creative minds began to explore the classic works of Greece and Rome for inspiration, turning away from the Christian culture that had dominated the arts and education since the fall of the Roman Empire in the West.

This Renaissance, or "rebirth," led to paintings, sculpture, and architecture that was based on Greek models. Artists also felt free to depict scenes from Greek mythology and contemporary everyday life, as the ancients had, instead of showing only Christian themes. In education, scholars read Plato, Aristotle, and the other Greeks and debated their ideas, finding that many of their ancient conclusions were still relevant. Petrarch (1304–1374), an Italian poet, played a key role in this revival. He was considered the first modern humanist—someone who places the study of human concerns above religion, just as the Greek philosophers had done centuries before. Petrarch tried to learn ancient Greek, and he encouraged other scholars to do the same. They took his advice, and for the next few hundred years educated people across Europe and the lands where Europeans settled learned ancient Greek so they could study the classics as they were written, and not in translation.

The rise of humanism led to a new interest in science, which had already been influenced by the translation of Greek works into Latin. The scientific method of the Greeks, based on reasoning and observation, was expanded to include experimentation. Scientists came up with a theory, based on existing knowledge, and then tested it to see if it was true. The scientific revolution that began in the 16th century drew upon the spirit of in-

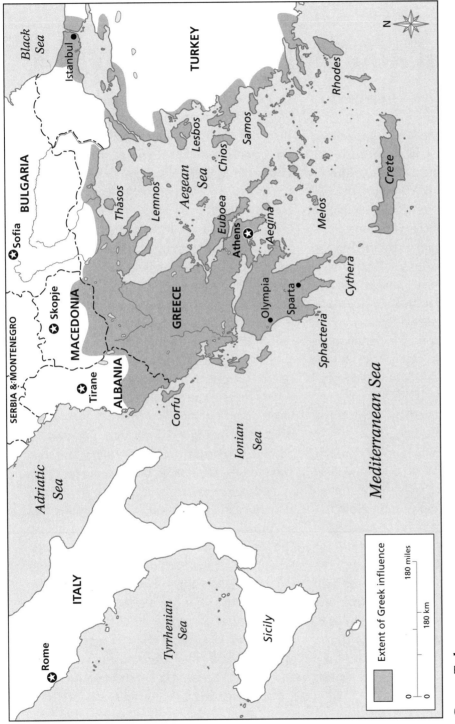

Greece Today
Greece and Turkey are the two largest modern nations that were once part of the ancient Greek empire.

The Parthenon Marbles Controversy

As in ancient times, the Parthenon still stands on a hill overlooking all of Athens, but it has gone through several transformations. After serving Greeks as a temple to Athena, it was used as a Christian church for about 500 years, then a mosque for Turkish Muslims, although almost all of the Greek population of about 10 million people has remained staunchly Christian.

The Parthenon was badly damaged in the late 1600s, when the Italian city-state of Venice controlled some of the Greek islands in the Ionian Sea and was attacking mainland Greece. The Turks used the Parthenon to store munitions, which exploded during the Venetian attack. The Parthenon was left a ruin. It was further altered in the early 1800s when British diplomat and art collector Thomas Bruce, Lord Elgin (1766–1841) removed the sculptured friezes from around the building.

In 1816 the British Museum in London purchased much of what was then called the Elgin Marbles from Elgin, who claimed he had taken them out of Greece to preserve them from further ruin. Some British writers, however, claimed that taking the sculptures defaced what was left of the Parthenon and that no one had a right to steal art, especially pieces that represented such as strong cultural legacy, no matter what reasons they gave for doing so. After World War II, some people suggested the British should give back the marbles to thank the Greeks for their resistance against Nazi Germany. The British government refused.

Interest in the issue was renewed in 1982 when Greek actress Melina Mercouri, who was then the Greek minister of culture, addressed the International Conference of Ministers of Culture in Mexico, pleading for the return of the friezes, now known as the Parthenon Marbles, to Athens.

A committee of British classics scholars was formed in 1983 to lobby for return of the sculptures to Greece, and more recently, in 2000, the Greek government proposed to the British House of Commons that more important than actual ownership of the Parthenon Marbles was their location: Should they not be as close to their original setting as possible? Still, some people argued that keeping the marbles in a British museum protects them from the high levels of air pollution in Athens. Besides, some officials claim, Elgin did not steal the marbles; he had permission from the ruling Ottoman Turks to take the statues, and he paid for them.

Today, a new Acropolis Museum is planned to protect and preserve all of the religious site's sculptures, including the Parthenon Marbles. The viewpoint of the British Committee for the Restitution of the Parthenon Marbles, according to their web site, is that "It is inconceivable that over half of its [the Parthenon's] celebrated sculptural elements should be exhibited 2,000 miles away from the . . . actual monument for which they were expressly designed and carved." So far, the British Museum's reply is that the marbles are staying in London.

quiry that motivated the Greeks, while leading to conclusions that disproved some Greek concepts. The old Ptolemaic system for explaining the universe, for example, did not survive. Polish scientist Nicholas Copernicus (1473–1543) suggested and Italian astronomer Galileo Galilei (1564–1642) proved that the sun was the center of our solar system, not the Earth. Galileo, however, did not have the same freedom as his ancient Greek counterparts, and the Roman Catholic Church forced the Italian astronomer to denounce what he knew to be true.

Controversial Art
Sculptures that form part of the Parthenon Marbles are now on display at the British Museum in London. There is an international movement to return them to Greece, but so far the British Museum says it will not give them up.

English and other European settlers who came to North America brought their knowledge of classical Greece and Rome with them. When American revolutionaries considered various forms of government, they held up classical Rome as an ideal. In the 18th century, most Americans did not want a direct democracy, as in the Athens of Pericles. They preferred a republic, as the Romans had, with men (and only men) who owned property electing others to create their laws. Still, many American and British thinkers admired features of the Greek political system.

Aristotle wrote extensively about the constitution of Athens, and Americans such as Samuel Adams saw that Great Britain had its own unwritten constitution that included laws dating back to the Magna Carta of the 13th century. That document placed limits on the monarchy's power in its relationship with Britain's aristocracy. Americans also saw that the British government featured three elements Aristotle had discussed: monarchy, aristocracy, and democracy (though not direct democracy). The men who governed after the American Revolution favored eliminating monarchy and limiting the aristocracy, giving the people–the *demos*–a greater role in the government. The U.S. leaders went one step further than the British and wrote a formal constitution, describing exactly what the government would include and how it would function. The Americans also created a Bill of Rights, spelling out individual freedoms that would be protected. These freedoms included some of the same ones the Greeks cherished–freedom of speech, freedom of religion, and the right to have a jury trial.

TIME LINE

1200S B.C.E.	Mycenaean culture reaches its high point. Troy is destroyed.
1100 B.C.E.	Struggles among Mediterranean cultures bring about Dark Age in the entire region. Mycenaean palaces are destroyed.
776 B.C.E.	As Greek civilization rebounds, the first Olympic games are held in Olympia.
750–700 B.C.E.	The Greek alphabet is developed. Homer's poetry is first written down.
750-550 B.C.E.	Greek colonization means new Greek city-states are formed throughout the Mediterranean and Black Sea areas.
630 B.C.E.	Sparta enslaves the defeated Messenians, who will serve as agricultural slaves for Sparta until they are freed by Thebes in the fourth century B.C.E.
600 B.C.E.	Hoplite infantry becomes common throughout Greece. Sappho writes poetry about the personal experience of love and longing.
594 B.C.E.	Solon reforms Athenian law and extends power to the lower classes.
C. 585–550 B.C.E.	The earliest Greek philosophers, Thales, Anaximander, and Anaximemes, present new ideas about the universe that have nothing to do with the gods.
508 B.C.E.	Cleisthenes puts Athens on clear path to democracy.
490 B.C.E.	Though greatly outnumbered, hoplites from Athens and Plataea defeat the army of the Persian Empire at Marathon to win the first Persian War.
480–479 B.C.E.	Greek victories in the second Persian War usher in the Athenian empire and the Classical period of Greek civilization, with enormous achievements in government, literature, drama, architecture, and art.
447–432 B.C.E.	The Parthenon is built in Athens.
431–404 B.C.E.	The Peloponnesian War is fought between Athens and Sparta and their allies.
399 B.C.E.	Athenian philosopher and teacher Socrates is executed.
370 B.C.E.	Thebes, under the leadership of Epiminondas, invades Sparta and frees the Messenian *helots*. (Epiminondas dies in a later Theban victory in 362 B.C.E.)
338 B.C.E.	Philip II of Macedon defeats a coalition of Greek forces and establishes the League of Corinth. After Philip's assassination in 336 B.C.E., his son Alexander the Great conquers the Persian Empire and Egypt.
331 B.C.E.	Alexander founds Alexandria in Egypt. It will become the capital of the far-ranging Greek-speaking world after his death.
323 B.C.E.	Alexander dies. Three Hellenistic kingdoms are established by his generals.
146 B.C.E.	The Roman Empire conquers Greece and Macedonia.

RESOURCES: Books

Evslin, Bernard, *Heroes, Gods and Monsters of the Greek Myths* (New York: Laurel Leaf, Reissue edition, 1984)

This compelling book introduces the wondrous and terrifying world of superhuman beings, such as Medusa and the Minotaur, and gods like Zeus, Athena, and Poseidon–brought to life through exciting retellings of great adventures.

Garland, Robert, *Daily Life of the Ancient Greeks* (Westport, Conn: Greenwood Press, 1998)

A vivid, engaging, and colorful description of life in ancient Greece from the perspective of ordinary people.

Glubok, Shirley, *Olympic Games in Ancient Greece* (New York: HarperCollins, 1976)

An account of the Olympic games as they probably occurred in 400 B.C.E.

Hamilton, Edith, *The Greek Way* (New York: W. W. Norton & Company, Reissue edition, 1993)

A highly readable introduction to the history and culture of ancient Greece, while giving the reader a closer look at some of the key intellectual figures in Classical Greek thought.

Homer (translated by Robert Fagles), *The Iliad and The Odyssey* (New York, Penguin Books, 1999)

These well-received translations of Homer's classics about war, heroism, gods, monsters, and returning home again are as compelling to read now as they were 3,000 years ago.

Osborne, Robin, *Archaic and Classical Greek Art* (New York: Oxford University Press, 1998)

This account of Greek art from about 800 to 323 B.C.E. shows how sculptors, painters, and artisans responded to the challenges of world in which the Greek city-state was created and developed. The author shows how artistic developments were an integral part of the intensely competitive life of the Greek city-state.

Pomeroy, Sarah B., Stanley M. Burstein, Walter Donlan, and Jennifer Tolbert Roberts, *Ancient Greece: A Political, Social, and Cultural History* (New York: Oxford University Press, 1999)

Ranging from Greece's beginnings in the Bronze Age through the tumultuous Hellenistic era dominated by Alexander the Great, this book presents a wide-ranging portrait of ancient Greece, including political, military, social and cultural history. The book is loaded with maps, photographs, and numerous document boxes that highlight a variety of primary source material.

Sacks, David, *Encyclopedia of the Ancient Greek World* (New York: Facts On File, 1995)

This readable, lively compendium of facts is presented in alphabetical entries that are logical, comprehensive, and cross-indexed. They include topics on history, politics, warfare and weaponry, social organizations, the arts, literature, language, mythology, geography, science and technology, clothing, religion, and more.

Skelton, Debra, and Pamela Dell, *Empire of Alexander the Great* (New York: Facts On File, 2005)

Learn more about the Hellenistic Age and how Alexander the Great, the Macedonian king, spread Greek civilization throughout the known world. This detailed look at Alexander's empire includes history, culture, religion, art, science, and everyday life.

RESOURCES: Web Sites

Ancient Greece
www.ancientgreece.com

This detailed and amply illustrated look at ancient Greece is divided into sections on history, architecture and art, geography, mythology, people, wars, and the Olympics. An extensive resources section is also included.

Ancient Greek Literature and Mythology
www.infoplease.com/spot/ancientgreece-lit-myth.html

This site from InfoPlease includes translations of plays, poetry, and literature, biographies of important figures, quizzes and games, heroes and legends, and an explanation of the references to Greek stories in the Harry Potter novels.

The Ancient Greek World
www.museum.upenn.edu/Greek_World

This site from the University of Pennsylvania Museum of Archaeology and Anthropology explores daily life, religion and death, art, economics and more. You can also take a virtual tour of an exhibit that explains how the ancient Greek, Roman, and Etruscan cultures intertwined.

The Ancient Olympics
www.perseus.tufts.edu/Olympics/

At this site, developed by the Classics department at Tufts University, you can compare ancient and modern Olympic sports, tour the site of Olympia as it looks today, learn about the context of the Games and the Olympic spirit, or read about the Olympic athletes who were famous in ancient times.

Art and Archaeology
www.perseus.tufts.edu/art&arch.html

Look through a massive library of art objects, sites, and buildings, including 523 coins, 1,548 vases, more than 1,400 sculptures, 179 archaeological and historical sites and 381 buildings. Each catalog entry has a description of the object and its context; most have images. Descriptions and images have been produced in collaboration with many museums, institutions and scholars.

British Committee for the Restitution of the Parthenon Marbles
www.parthenonuk.com

The committee's official web site contains detailed information on the Parthenon (Elgin) Marbles, together with the case for their return to Athens.

Elpenor: Home of the Greek Word
www.ellopos.net/elpenor/

Elpenor is a bilingual anthology of all periods of Greek literature, including downloadable versions of Plato, Aristotle and the New Testament of the Bible. Language pages feature lessons in ancient Greek, starting from the alphabet, continuing with Homer and combining grammar and syntax with an attempt to understand the value of the texts and of language itself for our life today. Amply illustrated with photographs and period art.

Exploring Plato's Dialogues
plato.evansville.edu

This web site from the University of Evansville features biographies and views of Plato and Aristotle.

The Greeks
www.pbs.org/empires/thegreeks

This multimedia web site, a companion to the PBS documentary "The Greeks: Crucible of Civilization," offers a lesson in ancient Greek, enables visitors to download a "virtual Socrates," or explore Athens with an interactive map, and includes a time line of Greek history.

BIBLIOGRAPHY

Adkins, Lesley, and Roy A. Adkins, *Handbook to Life in Ancient Rome*. New York: Oxford University Press, 1994.

Aristophanes, *Four Comedies*, Translated by Dudley Fitts. New York: Harcourt, Brace & World, 1962.

Atchity, Kenneth J., ed., *The Classical Greek Reader*. New York: Henry Holt and Company, 1996.

Boardman, John, Jasper Griffin, and Oswyn Murray, *The Oxford History of Greece and the Hellenistic World*. Oxford, U.K.: Oxford University Press, 1988.

Cahill, Thomas, *Sailing the Wine-Dark Sea: Why the Greeks Matter*. New York: Nan A. Talese/Doubleday, 2003.

Camp, John, and Elizabeth Fisher, *The World of the Ancient Greeks*. New York: Thames & Hudson, 2002.

Cantor, Norman, ed., *The Encyclopedia of the Middle Ages*. New York: Viking, 1999.

Cantor, Norman, and Peter L. Klein, eds., *Ancient Thought: Plato and Aristotle*. Waltham, Mass.: Blaisdell Publishing, 1969.

Cartledge, Paul, ed., *The Cambridge Illustrated History of Ancient Greece*. Cambridge, U.K.: Cambridge University Press, 1998.

"The Case for the Return." British Committee for the Restitution of the Parthenon Marbles. URL: http://www.parthenonuk.com/the_case_for_the_return.php. Accessed July 28, 2004.

Drabble, Margaret, ed., *The Oxford Companion to English Literature*, Revised ed. Oxford, U.K.: Oxford University Press, 1995.

Durant, Will, *The Life of Greece*. New York: Simon and Schuster, 1939.

Fine, John V. A., *The Ancient Greeks: A Critical History*. Cambridge, Mass.: Belknap Press,1983.

Finley, M I., *The Ancient Greeks*. New York: Viking Penguin, Inc. 1971.

———, *Economy and Society in Ancient Greece*. New York: Viking Press, 1981.

Flaceliere, Robert, *Daily Life in Greece at the Time of Pericles*. London: Phoenix Press, 1965.

Freeman, Charles, *The Greek Achievement: The Foundation of the Western World*. New York: Penguin Books, 1999.

Gardner, Helen, *Art Through the Ages*, Revised ed. New York: Harcourt Brace Jovanovich, 1975.

Garraty John A., and Peter Gay, eds., The Columbia History of the World. New York: Harper & Row, 1972.

Geanakoplos, Deno J., Medieval Western Civilization and the Byzantine and Islamic World. Lexington, Ky.: D.C. Heath and Company, 1979.

Grant, Michael, *The Founders of the Western World: A History of Greece and Rome*. New York: Charles Scribner's Sons, 1991.

Hamilton, Edith, *Mythology*. New York: Warner Books, 1942, 1969.

Hanson, Victor Davis, *The Wars of the Ancient Greeks*. New York: Sterling Publishing, 1999.

Harris, Nathaniel, *History of Ancient Greece*. New York: Barnes & Noble Books, 2000.

Herodotus, *The Histories*, Translated by Robin Waterfield. Oxford, U.K.: Oxford University Press,1998.

"Herodotus: Solon and Croesus," Ancient History Sourcebook. URL: http://www.fordham.edu/halsall/ancient/herodotus-creususandsolon.html. Accessed July 10, 2004.

Hesiod, "Works and Days." The Online Classical and Medieval Library. URL: http://sunsite.berkeley.edu/OMACL/Hesiod/works.html. Accessed July 24, 2004.

Honderich, Ted, ed., *The Oxford Companion to Philosophy*. Oxford, U.K.: Oxford University Press, 1995.

Hopper, R. J., *The Early Greeks*. New York: Harper & Row, 1976.

Hourani, Albert, *A History of the Arab Peoples*. Cambridge, MA: Belknap Press, 1991.

James, Peter, and Nick Thorpe, *Ancient Inventions*. New York: Ballantine Books, 1994.

Kaplan, Justin, ed., *Bartlett's Familiar Quotations*, 16th ed. Boston: Little, Brown and Company, 1992.

Long, Roderick T, "The Athenian Constitution." LewRockwell.com. URL: http://www.lewrockwell.com/long/long8.html. Accessed July 20, 2004.

Macrone, Michael, *By Jove!: Brush Up Your Mythology*. New York: Cader Books, 1992.

Martin, Thomas R., *Ancient Greece: From Prehistoric to Hellenistic Times*. New Haven, Conn.: Yale University Press, 2000.

Merriam Webster's Geographical Dictionary, 3rd ed. Springfield, Mass.: Merriam Webster, 1997.

National Public Radio, *All Things Considered* (transcripts), "Athens and Sparta Formalize Peace After 2,000 Years," hosted by Neal Conan, March 12, 1996.

National Public Radio, *Talk of the Nation* (transcripts), "Classical Education," hosted by Neal Conan, June 29, 1998.

"Olive Subsidies Threaten the Mediterranean Environment." WWF-UK. URL: http://www.wwf-uk.org/News/n_0000000290.asp. Posted June 18, 2001.

"The Parthenon of Nashville, Tennessee." Metropolitan Government of Nashville and Davidson County. URL: http://www.nashville.gov/parthenon. Accessed July 15, 2004.

Plato, *The Last Days of Socrates*, Translated by Hugh Tredennick. Middlesex, U.K.: Penguin Books, 1969.

Plato, *Symposium*, Translated by Benjamin Jowett. The Internet Classics Archive. URL: http://classics.mit.edu/Plato/symposium.html. Posted September 29, 2000.

Plautus, *Three Comedies*, Translated by Erich Segal. New York: Bantam Books, 1969.

Pollitt, J. J., *The Art of Ancient Greece: Sources and Documents*. Cambridge, U.K.: Cambridge University Press, 1990.

Pomeroy, Sarah B., Stanley M. Burstein, Walter Donlan, and Jennifer Tolbert Roberts, *Ancient Greece: A Political, Social, and Cultural History*. New York: Oxford University Press, 1999.

Pritchard, James B., ed., *The Harper Concise Atlas of the Bible*. New York: HarperCollins, 1991.

Quennell, Marjorie, and C. H. B. Quennell, *Everyday Things in Ancient Greece*, Revised by Kathleen Freeman. New York: G. P Putnam's Sons, 1965.

Shelley, Percy Bysshe, "Hellas." Poetry Archive. URL: http://www.poetry-archive.com/s/hellas.html. Posted 2002.

Strassler, Robert B., ed., *The Landmark Thucydides: A Comprehensive Guide to the Peloponnesian War*. New York: The Free Press, 1996.

Thucydides, *History of the Peloponnesian War*, Translated by Rex Warner. New York: Penguin Books, 1972.

Trichopoulou, Antonia, et al., "Adherence to a Mediterranean Diet and Survival in a Greek Population." *The New England Journal of Medicine*, June 26, 2003, Vol. 348:2599-2608.

Watkin, David, *A History of Western Architecture*, 2nd ed. London: Lawrence King, 1996.

Yaman, Ebru, "Music sleuth tracks down harps and lyres of ancients." *The Australian*, April 16, 2003.

Zimmerman, J.E., *Dictionary of Classical Mythology*. New York: Bantam Books, 1964.

INDEX

Page numbers in *italics* refer to captions for illustrations.